BASIC TELEMARKETING
Skills for Sales and Service Productivity

MARY D. PEKAS

Consulting Editor: **Dr. Rosemary T. Fruehling**
Editorial Director: **Mel Hecker**
Project Editor: **Paul A. Larson**
Writing/Editorial Services: **The Oldham Publishing Service**
Cover Design: **Herb Youner**
Illustrations: **Karen Badger** pp. 9, 29, 47, 52, 81, 91, 98, 107, 173, 192
 ©**Dynamic Graphics, Inc.**, pp. 50–55
 TOPS 18, 121, 123, 124, 127, 148
 Alice Porter Unit openers.

Library of Congress Cataloging–in–Publication Data
Pekas, Mary D.
 Basic Telemarketing.

 1. Telemarketing. I. Title.
HF5415.1265.P45 1989   658.8′4   89-10822
ISBN 0-574-20180-7

Copyright © 1990 by Paradigm Publishing International
6436 City West Parkway, Eden Prairie, MN 55344

All rights reserved. No part of this publication may be reproduced, stored in a retrieval system, or transmitted in any form or by any means, electronic, mechanical, photocopying, recording, or otherwise, without the prior written permission of Paradigm Publishing International.

Printed in the United States of America

10 9 8 7 6 5 4 3 2 1

BASIC TELEMARKETING
Skills for Sales and Service Productivity

Table of Contents

Introduction	vii
Chapter 1 Defining Telemarketing	**3**
Kinds of Telemarketing	4
A Growing Industry	6
Careers in Telemarketing	6
Telemarketing Modes	7
Outbound and Inbound Calls	9
Titles for Telemarketing Professionals	11
Vocabulary	11
Discussion Questions	12
Activities	13
Chapter 2 Identifying Elements of Telemarketing	**15**
Prospect/Customer Types	16
Telemarketing Maintenance Goals	16
Five Basic Types of Call	19
Structure of a Telemarketing Call	21
Telemarketing Records	39
Vocabulary	39
Discussion Questions	40
Activities	41
Chapter 3 Analyzing Strategies and Call Purposes	**43**
Telemarketing Strategies	44
Primary and Secondary Call Purposes	47

Matching Call Purposes to Career Paths — 48
Telemarketing Implementation Methods — 55
Human Resource Configurations — 57
Vocabulary — 59
Discussion Questions — 60
Activities — 60

Chapter 4 Using Scripts and Prompters — 63

Knowing Your Company — 64
Learning Scripts and Prompters — 66
Preparing Prompters — 69
Sample Script: Market Survey — 71
Vocabulary — 72
Discussion Questions — 72
Activities — 72

Chapter 5 Developing Service-Oriented Skills — 77

Effective Use of Telephone Equipment — 78
Procedure for All Calls — 81
Procedure for Inbound Calls — 86
Procedure for Outbound Calls — 89
Vocabulary — 93
Discussion Questions — 93
Activities — 94

Chapter 6 Developing a Positive Attitude — 97

Attitude and Persistence — 98
Two Control Factors — 101
Two Steps to Change Your Thinking Mood — 104
Three Kinds of Affirmations — 105
Complaints — 108
Vocabulary — 113
Discussion Questions — 113
Activities — 114

Chapter 7 Keeping Records — 117

- Essential for Service — 118
- Record Management System — 118
- Call Tracking Equipment — 119
- Note-taking Techniques — 127
- Complaints — 129
- Call Preparation — 131
- Vocabulary — 131
- Discussion Questions — 131
- Activities — 132

Chapter 8 Using Words Effectively — 135

- Not All Words Are Created Equal — 136
- Context — 137
- Connotation — 138
- Categories — 139
- Pronunciation — 145
- Articulation — 146
- Vocabulary — 149
- Discussion Questions — 149
- Activities — 150

Chapter 9 Creating Your Own Style — 155

- Soft Sell vs. Hard Sell — 156
- Conversational vs. Formal — 160
- Vocabulary — 163
- Discussion Questions — 163
- Activities — 164

Chapter 10 Establishing Your Tone — 169

- Lacking Visual Clues — 170
- Aspects of Telephone Delivery — 171
- Reaching the Mind's Eye — 172
- What Is in a Tone? — 172

What Is Pitch?	174
Factors Affecting Pitch	175
Rate of Speech	178
Volume	180
Vocabulary	182
Discussion Questions	182
Activities	183

Chapter 11 Adding Zest to Your Voice — 187

Using Your Voice to Add Emphasis	188
Various Kinds of Emphasis	188
Pause to Emphasize	189
Inflection	190
Sample Script	193
Vocabulary	194
Discussion Questions	194
Activities	195

Chapter 12 Listening to Communicate — 199

What Is Listening?	200
Better Listening, Better Results	201
Internal Obstacles to Listening	203
External Obstacles to Listening	204
Helping Your Ears	205
Vocabulary	213
Discussion Questions	214
Activities	214

Glossary — 217

Index — 229

Introduction

Basic Telemarketing

Telemarketing began with the first telephone call, which was made by Alexander Graham Bell. His telephone dialog was, "Watson, come here, I need you." In telemarketing terminology, we would refer to Bell's call as an outbound telemarketing call for service. From that beginning, the use of the telephone has continued to increase in both business and consumer applications.

This course in basic telemarketing will provide a solid foundation for students who want training in the professional use of the telephone for sales and service, referred to in the industry as telesales and teleservice.

The Basic Telemarketing course is based on a system of telemarketing training, which was developed during 20 years of practical telemarketing experience by Mary Pekas, president and founder in 1982 of Telemarketing Institute, Inc. Clients of Telemarketing Institute include Northwestern Bell, Honeywell, Northwest Banks, Lutheran Brotherhood, General Electric, and Nielsen Market Research.

Ms. Pekas teaches telemarketing as talking on the phone in a natural, casual, friendly manner, as you would face-to-face with a friend, to give the person with whom you are talking the opportunity courteously, with no feeling of being pressured, to choose to buy what is being offered.

This approach to telemarketing uses carefully selected words and positive voice qualities to project a genuine, service-oriented attitude to create a comfortable business atmosphere.

This system of telemarketing involves using contractions so you sound casual and friendly, not stiff and formal; using courteous ways of presenting points of interest so you'll be persuasive, not "hard sell;" preceding outbound calls with notes of introduction whenever possible; always proceeding only with permission through the steps of the sale; and always asking permission to call in the future and calling only when permission is granted.

For businesses, this approach results in the building of a large prospect base and a list of loyal, satisfied customers. For the telephone sales/service representatives (referred to as TSRs) there is little rejection and stress, and they are able to experience pride and self-fulfillment in their career.

Sometimes, when TSRs use telephone dialogs prepared by someone else and are instructed to follow them to the letter, they sound to the listener that they are reading a script or giving a "canned pitch," which *can* cause the listener to tune out. *Basic Telemarketing* trains each person to use his or her own comfortable personal language and to speak in the key of "B Natural." This is the reason the system suggests the use of contractions and informal, nontechnical words that have non-pressure psychological effects.

You will be taught to use such phrases as "May I share with you..." in place of "Let me tell you...." The former has a softer tone compared with the harsh sound of the latter. Just as the actual sound is softer in "May I share with you...," the psychological implications are more soft sell than "Let me tell you...." No one likes to be "told."

The major difference between face-to-face selling and telemarketing is the lack of visual image in the latter. Learning of the tremendous impact that visual feedback has on effective communication in face-to-face situations was a breakthrough in the author's research on identifying the element that creates a comfortable business atmosphere on the telephone for both the caller and the person being called.

For 10 years, before starting her company, the author was asked to work with people, privately, to help them develop phone selling skills and to overcome their dislike of the phone and sometimes outright fear of dialing a number. Some people had such fear of the phone that they broke out in rashes and their hands shook. Some, even those who otherwise had perfect diction, stammered, stuttered, or mouthed words without making a sound.

The author had spent six to eight hours a day on the phone for 17 years selling products, services, and appointments, loved it and experienced great job satisfaction. The challenge was understanding and relating to the fear and dislike other people exhibited. "I wanted to identify why I liked phoning so much while others feared it enough to have these drastic physical reactions."

She kept a list of the reasons people gave for their dislike that might reveal a common denominator. She used this information to develop a training program that would help people overcome their fear and allow them to enjoy their work and be productive telemarketing professionals.

The unease and fear stemmed from the fact that both the caller and the person being called found themselves outside of their "comfort zones" because of the missing visual image. The visual image needed to be replaced by skills that many people have not developed highly—the skill of using their voice effectively.

Using their voice effectively involves developing a positive attitude as well as selecting the right words. It involves projecting an interest-holding tone and it also involves the important art of listening. The effective use of the voice compensates for the missing visual image and puts the human element into telemarketing. This understanding of the need to compensate for the missing visual image in order to inject the human element into telephoning forms the basis of this course.

Drawing on her many years of experience, the author developed a telemarketing system that places the emphasis on the human element. It is built around a totally non-pressure philosophy. Telemarketing sales representatives using this system create a non-pressure, friendly, business atmosphere by developing a telephone style that integrates the skills of conversation and listening. This approach generates a comfort zone conducive to acceptance and trust by creating a comfortable business atmosphere in which all pressure and rejection from the phone call is removed for both parties.

Those using this approach will have an enjoyable job with low rejection. TSRs will develop trust and rapport, which leads to consistency in sales.

The approach creates a comfortable work environment and cuts down on stress and burnout, thereby reducing turnover and saving time and money in hiring and training new employees. The result for companies is increased revenue and new accounts without large increases in selling expense.

Considerable legislation regarding telemarketing is pending in the United States. This legislation is concerned with discourteous, high pressure sales approaches, and the use of computer calling. The non-pressure, courteous approach taught in *Basic Telemarketing* eliminates the concern of having to deal with legislative actions and adds the needed element of professionalism to telemarketing.

This textbook combines theory and practical information as well as various activities to practice and develop the skills taught. An accompanying workbook provides the opportunity for you to apply and sharpen your newly acquired skills in simulated situations that reflect actual work environments.

As you go through this course, you'll learn more about the psychological implications of many words and phrases, and you will receive suggestions for developing your own conversational style.

Unit I
INTRODUCTION TO TELEMARKETING

Chapter 1—Defining Telemarketing

Chapter 2—Identifying Elements of Telemarketing

Chapter 3—Analyzing Strategies and Call Purposes

Chapter 4—Using Scripts and Prompters

Kinds of Telemarketing

A Growing Industry

Careers in Telemarketing

Telemarketing Modes

Outbound and Inbound Calls

Titles for Telemarketing Professionals

Vocabulary

Discussion Questions

Activities

Chapter 1

Defining Telemarketing

Upon completion of this chapter, you will be able to

- define telemarketing,
- identify four telemarketing career paths,
- define the two major telemarketing modes,
- identify the two broad categories of telemarketing calls,
- recognize four telemarketing titles.

The word "telemarketing" was coined in 1967 by C. Dickey Dyer, III, a consultant in the distribution/wholesale industry. The public became aware of the word in 1978, through a Bell Systems advertisement, and generally believed that the business world had discovered a new use of the telephone. Telemarketing, however, is not a new way of doing business. It is simply a new word to describe an old business activity previously called "phone work." Professional telemarketing involves an extension of traditional, tested business uses of the telephone in a systematic, deliberate manner. While telemarketing can include many different business uses, this course defines telemarketing as communicating by telephone to sell customers or prospective customers on something—an idea, a company image, a product, a service or an appointment—and servicing customer complaints and questions. (Throughout this text the phrase prospect/customer will be used when the techniques or applications can apply equally well to both prospects and customers.)

Eugene B. Kordahl, president of National Telemarketing, Inc., defines telemarketing as "the planned use of the telephone in conjunction with traditional marketing methods and techniques."

Kinds of Telemarketing

Selling and *marketing* are two terms you will see frequently in this text. People often use them as though they meant the same thing, and the goal of both is to produce revenue by encouraging a prospect or customer to purchase a product or service. The industry recognizes a difference between selling and marketing, however.

Marketing refers to the effort to create a favorable atmosphere for the sale of a product or service, rather than the sale itself. This can involve newspaper advertisements, television commercials,

---

Many people, including those in business, remain uncertain of exactly what telemarketing is. This was demonstrated by an independent survey conducted by Rob Valesco and Dan Giebert, senior business majors at Augustana College, Sioux Falls, S.D. The survey was designed to find out how many business people used telemarketing in their businesses and how many knew that was what they were doing.

To the question "Do you do telemarketing in your business?" only 10 percent of the business owners replied "Yes."

Forty-six percent of the companies, however, also said "Yes" to at least one of the following questions: "Do you have anyone arranging appointments by phone?" "Does your business have an 800 number?" "Do you have a customer service department [to handle telephone calls]?"

All of these are telemarketing activities. Thus, while 46 percent of the companies were actively engaged in telemarketing, only 10 percent were aware that was what they were doing.

> The telephone is so named by its inventor, A. G. Bell. He believes that one day they will be installed in every residence and place of business. Bell's profession is that of a voice teacher, yet he claims to have discovered an instrument of great practical value and communication which has been overlooked by thousands of workers who have spent years in the field. Bell's proposal to place his instrument in almost every home and business place is fantastic. The central exchange alone would represent a huge outlay in real estate and buildings, to say nothing of the electrical equipment. In conclusion, the committee feels it must advise against any investment in Bell's scheme. We do not doubt that it will find users in special circumstances, but any development of the kind and scale which Bell so fondly imagined is utterly out of the question."
>
> Excerpted from a report of a Western Union committee that met in 1877, when Alexander Graham Bell first came to them with some of his ideas for the application of his telephone.

direct mail (brochures, letters or other material mailed directly from the company), and telemarketing calls.

Selling refers to direct efforts to sell a specific product or service to a specific prospect or customer. This effort can include the clerk in a store waiting on a customer, the salesperson in a showroom, the door-to-door or office-to-office salesperson, and, again, telemarketing calls.

To some people, telemarketing suggests a "boiler room" operation in which wall-to-wall phone workers disturb people at home during the dinner hour to sell shoddy products or fly-by-night services, using high-pressure tactics. This may happen, but it is not legitimate, professional telemarketing.

Legislation to regulate telemarketing is pending in the United States. This legislation aims at the discourteous, high-pressure sales approaches and the use of computers to make calls. The non-pressure, courteous approach that you will be taught in this course reduces the need for such legislation because it is not an intrusion by a fast-talking salesperson or, even worse, an impersonal machine.

Legitimate, professional telemarketing performs many needed services. It provides information easily and quickly to those who want it. By helping to reduce sales costs, it helps to keep prices down. It offers a source of quick help when purchasers need it.

A Growing Industry

Telemarketing is affecting our economy in positive ways. It is generating increased sales of products and services. It has made a particularly significant impact on the job market through the creation of more jobs—jobs that provide greater employment opportunities for the handicapped, either sex, people over 62, the disadvantaged, the displaced, and minorities. It also generates dollars for other industries.

In the 1960s, Mona Ling, author of *How to Put Yourself Across Over The Phone*, pointed out that 90 percent of all businesses conduct some of their business over the phone. Her observation remains as valid as ever today, if not more so. Soon, 90 percent of all businesses will conduct an *extensive* part of their business over the phone.

In recent years, telemarketing has grown rapidly. A key factor in its growth is the rising cost of face-to-face sales calls, which is currently close to $300 per call. A telemarketing call is considerably cheaper—even one across the country. Furthermore, you can make several telemarketing calls in the time required for one face-to-face call.

> A forecast of which businesses will create the most jobs in the next decade adapted from one printed in *U.S. News & World Report* of May 9, 1983, shows telemarketing leading the list.
>
> **Jobs Created by Year 2000 (in millions)**
>
> | | |
> |---|---|
> | Telesales/teleservice workers | 8.0 |
> | CAD/CAM (computer aided design and manufacturing) | 1.2 |
> | Software writers | 1.0 |
> | Geriatric social workers | 0.6 |
> | Housing-rehabilitation workers | 0.49 |
> | Energy, conservation technicians | 0.4 |
> | Emergency medical technicians | 0.375 |

Careers in Telemarketing

You can think of the different types of telemarketing as four career paths to consider when planning your future in the industry. When doing so it is useful to think in terms of *telesales*, *teleservice*, *teleorder*, and *market research*. As you read and learn more about these different types of telemarketing, think of your own personality and needs to determine which will most suit you.

Telesales includes efforts to sell products and services, arrange appointments, and sell ideas. This is a good career path for those with a strong interest in sales.

Teleservice and teleorder (no selling) involves making or receiving calls for customer service, which includes order entry, providing information on products and services, answering questions and giving assistance to customers, handling complaints, and so on. This is a good career path for service-oriented people.

Teleservice and teleorder (with selling) means service calls that can be expanded to include sales activity. This is a rewarding career path for those interested in both sales and service tasks.

Teleservice also includes **market research** work, which involves making calls for information, rather than providing a service or making sales.

Telemarketing Modes

When a company considers telemarketing, it has two options:

- set up an in-house telemarketing operation, or
- hire the services of an outside telemarketing company.

In-House Telemarketing

Any company whose telemarketing operation calls for repeated, ongoing phone contact with the same prospects/customers, or that sells a technical product, will usually choose to set up its telemarketing operation in-house. This allows management to supervise the telemarketing project firsthand.

Some types of companies that would often opt for an in-house operation would be insurance companies, banks, mail order firms, manufacturers of appliances, and credit card companies.

Because they are inside the company, these operations are referred to as **"in-house telemarketing"** operations. These operations are sometimes called **inside sales**, to distinguish them from **outside sales**, in which people make sales and service calls on the outside. The term "inside sales," however, includes many other people besides those in telemarketing—clerks in all retail stores—so "in-house telemarketing" is used for activities exclusive to telemarketing.

An in-house telemarketing operation does not necessarily have a specific location and separate department within a company, but it is a telemarketing operation that has been planned, organized, and implemented.

In-house telemarketing operations vary in size, from one person making and/or receiving calls at a desk in a general office, to a special telemarketing department with its own room(s) filled with people in sound-proof telemarketing stations (also referred to as **telemods**) using the latest telecommunication equipment.

Telemarketing Service Bureau (TSB)

Many companies go outside their own organization and hire a **telemarketing service bureau** or **TSB** to do their telemarketing for them. The telemarketing service bureau does not conduct other business. It is created and organized to carry out telemarketing for others. As a TSB, it hires and trains TSRs to make and/or receive a wide variety of telemarketing calls for many different businesses.

Response Centers

The TSB contracts with client companies to do their calling for them or to act as their response center for **800 number** (toll-free) **call-in inquiries** (calls for information, to ask for literature, or to place an order).

As a part of their service, many TSBs consult with their clients and help design a telemarketing approach. The TSB monitors and tracks all calls and provides clients with comprehensive reports regarding call effectiveness and results.

Number of Calls

The number of contact calls that a company expects to need for its chosen telemarketing method will largely determine whether it sets up its own in-house telemarketing operation or uses the services of a TSB. Other factors influencing the decision include the frequency of calls and the cost of in-house telemarketing as opposed to that of a TSB.

Companies engage TSBs mostly for one-time projects, such as a special sale or an annual fund raiser, for trade show follow-up or help during a peak season, and for short-term *lead generation projects* and *market surveys*. **Lead generation projects** are designed to develop a list of prospective customers that can be called on later—by telephone or in person. In a **market survey** many

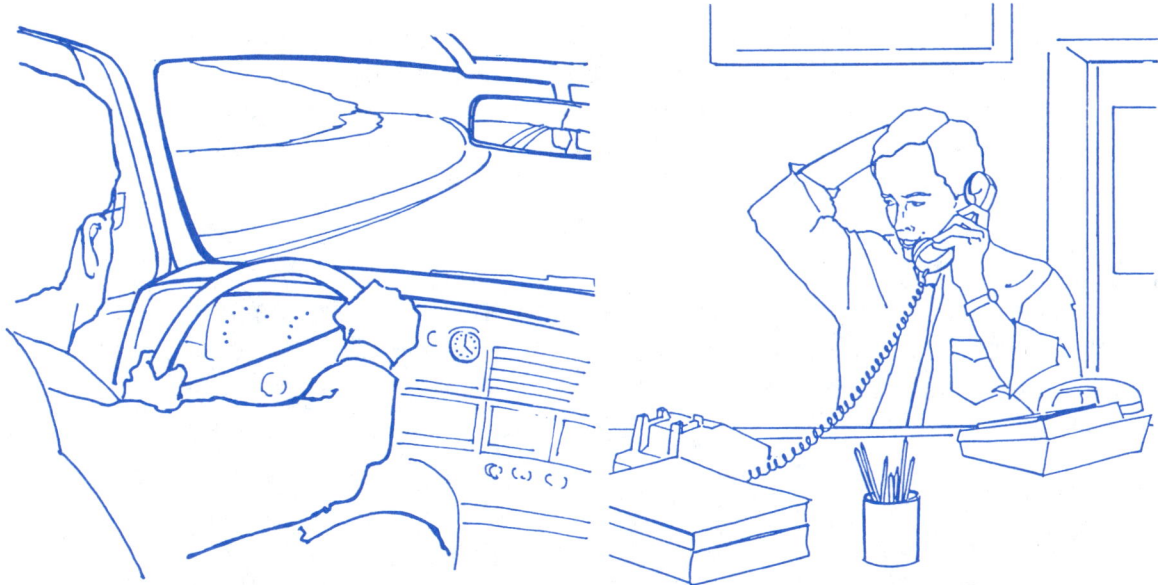

The increasing cost of making face-to-face calls has made telemarketing popular.

people are called and asked their opinion on a particular product or service to determine a potential market.

Outbound and Inbound Calls

Telemarketing revolves around two broad categories of calls: outbound and inbound. Besides the obvious ones, there are subtle differences in these calls with which you as a telemarketing professional will need to be familiar.

In Chapter 5 you will learn techniques for handling these different kinds of calls. Here is a general definition of each.

Outbound Call (O)

An **outbound call** is one made by a Telephone Sales/Service Representative (TSR) to a prospect or customer, to offer a product or service for sale, to arrange an appointment or to sell an idea, or to perform a business service.

This type of call is sometimes referred to as a **proactive call** because the representative takes the initiative to make the call.

In keeping records, the worker would identify this type of call with the letter "O."

Inbound Call (I)

An **inbound call** is one initiated by the prospect/customer to place an order, seek information, register a complaint, or conduct some other business. The inbound call is sometimes referred to as a **reactive call** because the representative receiving the call reacts to the caller by taking appropriate action. For record management, this call is identified with the letter "I."

Job descriptions for telephone sales/service representatives (TSRs) vary according to the type of operation in which they work. Regardless of the variations, however, all TSRs have similar basic responsibilities. Here is a sample job description of the basic responsibilities.

TSR Job Description

Objective: To sell or set up appointments to sell a company's product or service to existing and new customers; to provide service and information as required to customers and prospects.

Function: To make outbound calls to and/or handle inbound calls from prospects/customers four hours to eight hours a day; maintain telemarketing call records.

Tasks:

Call Preparation—obtaining numbers, checking names, preparing presentation (at least 15 minutes at beginning of each calling session).

Make calls—50 minutes out of each hour.

Maintain call record sheets and other required written records.

Prepare sales presentations.

Write scripts, telephone dialog prompters.

Know, and remain up-to-date on, company products/services.

Attend training sessions.

Take orders accurately.

Handle complaints politely and quickly.

Make necessary follow-up calls.

Maintain a courteous telephone manner.

Keep an uncluttered, efficient work station.

Titles for Telemarketing Professionals

"Tele" is a Greek word that means distant. "Phone" is a Greek word meaning sound. Alexander Graham Bell combined the two to make telephone—a device to send sound over a distance. We are so familiar with the word Mr. Bell coined, the word telemarketing makes sense because it conveys the idea of selling over a telephone.

Many titles have been coined for people making or receiving telemarketing calls. Some are specific titles that combine the prefix "tele-" with other words, just as the words telephone and telemarketing were formed. Common examples are:

- **Telesalesperson**—A person who sells products/services.

- **Telecollector**—A person who collects past due accounts.

- **Teleaccount Representative** or **Teleaccount Executive**—A person who sells to and services select customers.

Telephone Sales/Service Representative is a general title for anyone making or receiving sales or service calls. It can be shortened to *Telephone Service Representative* or *Telephone Sales Representative*, depending on the type of calls being handled. This general title is abbreviated "TSR."

- **Telephone Service Representative** (TSR)—A person who takes customer service and order entry calls or makes service-oriented calls.

- **Telephone Sales Representative** (TSR)—A person who uses the phone to sell a product, service, or equipment. The term includes people who make outbound calls and people who receive inbound sales calls.

Vocabulary

800 Number	Reactive Call
Call-in Inquiry	Selling
Direct Mail	Teleaccount Executive
In-house Telemarketing	Teleaccount Representative
Inbound Call	Telecollector
Inside Sales	Telemarketing Service Bureau (TSB)
Lead Generation Project	Telemod
Market Research	Telephone Sales Representative (TSR)
Market Survey	Telephone Service Representative (TSR)

Marketing
Outbound call
Outside Sales
Proactive Call
Telesales
Telesalesperson
Teleservice /Teleorder (no selling)
Teleservice/Teleorder (with selling)

Discussion Questions

1. What is telemarketing? Does everyone who uses telemarketing techniques know they are doing so?

2. What is the difference between selling and marketing?

3. Why do some people feel uncomfortable with the idea of telemarketing?

4. How is telemarketing affecting the economy? Why has it grown so quickly?

5. What are the two major modes of telemarketing? How do they differ?

6. Who might have an in-house telemarketing department? Who might use a TSB? Explain answer.

7. What is the difference between inbound and outbound calls?

8. What are four telemarketing career paths?

9. What are four telemarketing titles?

10. What is one general title that can refer to anyone engaged in telemarketing work? What two titles can it be shortened to? How is it abbreviated?

Activities

A. Identifying Career Paths

This activity will help you to identify telemarketing career paths and increase your awareness of telemarketing activities in local businesses.

Look for the employment section in your local newspaper. Bring to class this section from several issues, including a Sunday issue, for discussion. Look at the job openings under the headings marketing, sales, and telemarketing. Try to match the jobs to the different telemarketing career paths described in this chapter. Do they indicate what kind of telemarketing calls are involved? If they do not, can you think what kind of calls would be required?

B. Describing Basic Telemarketing Goals

This activity will help you to understand the two basic goals of telemarketing and its two major modes.

Look at the yellow pages of your local phone book and select businesses that might use telemarketing. Decide whether they use the phone for marketing or for selling, or for both. Decide which of the two major telemarketing modes best describes each business. Write down your decisions to discuss in the classroom.

Prospect/Customer Types

Telemarketing Maintenance Goals

Five Basic Types of Call

Structure of a Telemarketing Call

Telemarketing Records

Vocabulary

Discussion Questions

Activities

Chapter 2

Identifying Elements of Telemarketing

Upon completion of this chapter, you will be able to

- distinguish between the two prospect/customer types,
- define the two basic maintenance goals of a telemarketing operation,
- identify five basic types of telemarketing calls,
- describe the seven parts of a telemarketing call.

This chapter describes and defines the elements of the telemarketing industry to give you a clear picture of how these elements fit together. Telemarketing operations have two basic goals: attract new customers and service existing customers.

Specific types of telemarketing calls can be identified, and all telemarketing calls have definite, identifiable parts.

Prospect/Customer Types

Prospects and customers in telemarketing can be divided into two main categories: businesses and individuals. As with inbound and outbound calls, there are obvious and subtle differences between these two categories.

Business to Business

Business-to-business telemarketing consists of one business calling another business during business hours to offer goods and services and arrange appointments. Business-to-business telemarketing at present constitutes more than two-thirds of all telemarketing and is the most widely accepted kind.

Business to Consumer

Business-to-consumer telemarketing consists of a business calling individuals in their homes. Business-to-consumer telemarketing calls are made mostly for one of two basic reasons: to present products, services, or ideas to prospects/customers over the phone, and to arrange appointments for outside salespeople, who will meet with prospects/customers later to present products, services, and ideas for their consideration.

Telemarketing Maintenance Goals

Maintenance goals is a phrase used in psychology for those activities that a group must carry out to exist—to maintain itself. Telemarketing operations have two maintenance goals:

1. continually develop new prospect lists and

2. service and keep existing customers. (Note that customers are sometimes referred to as *accounts*.)

Prospect Development

Prospect development involves building a large **prospect base** (list of potential customers), and gradually converting prospects into customers by carrying out prospect follow-up. (**Follow-up** means making subsequent calls, with the prospect's permission, to keep in touch and to address specific needs he or she may have.)

This consists of identifying prospect needs, determining call purposes based on those needs, and then making prepared phone calls to the prospect. A **call purpose** is the identified reason for making a call—the objective to be accomplished. (You will read about call purposes in Chapter 3.)

The TSR uses polite persistence, which means that he or she always asks permission to touch base by phone again within a reasonable period of time. Most prospects will agree to another call. These repeat calls are important. Studies show that 75 to 80 percent of all new business comes after the fifth call. (You will read more about the importance of repeat calls in Chapter 6.)

Customer Account Management

Customer account management has as its maintenance goal servicing and keeping a large, strong customer base. A **customer base** refers to all the current customers. There are three customer account management methods. A company may use only one method or combine two or three, depending on company size, number of TSRs, and number of prospects/customers. The customer account management methods are:

1. Complete Account Management

2. Major/Marginal Account Management

3. Credit Account Management

Complete Account

In the complete account management method, a TSR handles all the needs of assigned customers. The TSR makes and receives all calls for these accounts, takes orders, handles complaints, carries out follow-up calls, and monitors accounts for such things as late payments. Responsibilities for each assigned customer include:

- making telephone contacts at mutually agreed upon times;

- making face-to-face contact, if necessary or desired by customer or management, and if customer location makes it possible;

- responding to inbound customer calls for service, order placement, or complaints;

- making collection calls on past-due accounts.

Strong lines of trust and confidence are built when one TSR handles all the aspects of an account. In this situation even making calls about a past-due account becomes a natural flow of business that is comfortable for both the TSR and the customer. In complete account management, accounts vary in dollar volume and activity, but regardless of size, they remain with a TSR for handling.

Major/Marginal Account

As its name implies, major/marginal account management identifies the major and marginal customer accounts and assigns them accordingly: major ones to one TSR or group of TSRs and marginal ones to another TSR or group of TSRs. Each type of account requires its own special care. TSRs with good prospect development skills can be assigned to the marginal accounts. Once they have been built up, these accounts can be handed over to TSRs who are servicing the major accounts. Any commission is shared.

A **commission** is a percentage of the total amount of the sale. TSRs often receive commissions and **bonuses** (extra payments for reaching a certain goal), in addition to their regular salary or wage, to motivate performance.

Usually there are fewer major accounts. The rule of thumb is that 20 percent of the accounts brings in 80 percent of the revenue, and 80 percent brings in only 20 percent of the revenue.

This is an example of the **80/20 rule**. An Italian economist, Vilfredo Pareto, formulated this rule in the last century. According to him, the significant elements in any grouping make up only 20 percent of the total. That is, you can predict that 20 percent of your effort will bring in 80 percent of your results.

An example might be your stock portfolio. If you owned 100 shares of IBM stock and 2,000 shares of the Fly By Night Airline, your revenue would probably be around 80 percent from IBM and 20 percent from Fly By Night Airline.

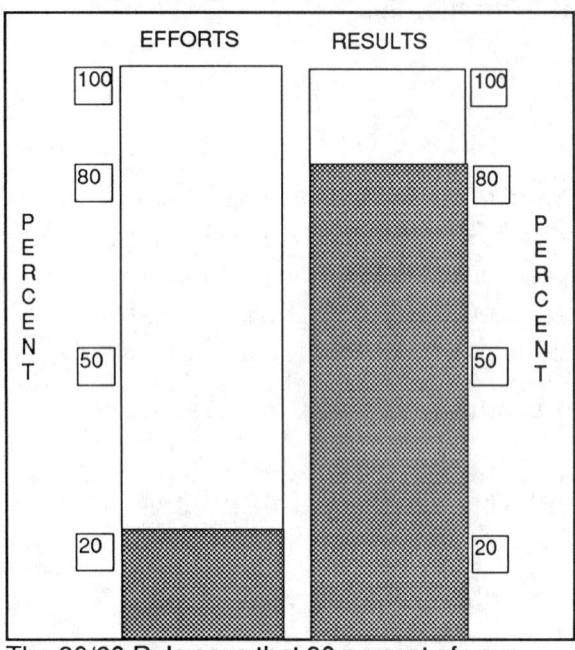

The 80/20 Rule says that 80 percent of your results come from 20 percent of your efforts.

Elements of Telemarketing   19

To set up a major/marginal account management system, a company:

- identifies major accounts as the top 20 percent of its customers and marginal accounts as the other 80 percent;

- assigns, according to a TSR's job description, the major and marginal accounts. A **job description** is a summary of the functions, tasks, and skills required in a job.

Credit Account

In credit account management, TSRs make calls on all aspects of credit. This can easily be a full-time position in large companies. Credit account management includes:

- *Screening Applications for Credit*—Calls to check or verify a prospect/customer request for new or additional credit.

- *Telecollection Service*—Making calls to keep accounts current. Planned, scheduled calls, made when an account is only slightly overdue and the dollar amount is small, are less stressful for both the TSR and the customer. It is thus easier to work out payment arrangements that will maintain customer satisfaction and keep accounts current.

- *Soliciting Credit Applications*—Making calls to encourage customers to apply for credit. (When customers are given the opportunity to charge, they almost always increase their purchase volume.)

Five Basic Types of Call

All telemarketing calls can be divided into five basic types: the *product/service sales call*, the *appointment call*, the *idea call*, the *service and order entry call*, and the *market research call*. These types can be grouped according to the career paths you read about in Chapter 1, and which you will read more about in Chapter 3.

Sales

Three types of call correspond to the first career path—telesales—and are referred to as **sales calls**. They are:

1. **Product/Service Sales Call**—A call to sell a *product* or a *service*. **Products** are goods that belong to the customer once they have been sold. They can be tangible, like furniture, appliances, or automobiles;

or intangible, like insurance policies. **Services** are tasks performed for a customer, either once or on a regular basis. They are intangible, but may involve the use of a product. Services include such things as office or house cleaning, lawn care, child care, or tax preparation.

2. **Appointment Call**—A call to arrange an appointment with a prospect. The TSR "sells" the prospect on the idea of an appointment. When prospects grant an appointment for a visit by phone or in person, they are far more receptive than they are to **cold calls**—ones made with no appointment.

3. **Idea Call**—A call made to convince prospects to try something. The sale of an idea calls for persuasive skills. It is usually business to consumer related rather than business to business. Ideas of giving money—to alumni foundations or political causes. Ideas of giving time—volunteering. Idea of paying past due bills—telecollection.

Service

The second and third career paths—teleservice and order entry with sales and with no sales—both involve the *service call*. In the first, the service call is combined with a sales call. In the second, the TSR makes only service calls and does not do any selling.

4. **Service and Order Entry Call**—Any call a company makes or receives that helps a customer. Do not confuse a *service call* with a *service sales call*, as defined above. A *service call* is to help customers who have made a purchase or who want to make a purchase and have called for information or some other kind of help. The service call is often a follow-up call to one a customer has made. Follow-up calls are an important part of the service-oriented approach, which keeps customers and gains new ones.

Market Research

Finally, there is market research, which does not involve any sales or service.

5. **Market Research Call**—A call to evaluate the market for a product or service. Specially prepared questionnaires are often used. TSRs record answers for analysis by management or another company.

Structure of a Telemarketing Call

An essential element of any telemarketing call is the sales presentation. The **presentation** is the overall *plan* for the call. Whether the call is inbound or outbound, a sales call, an appointment call, or an idea call, it will always be carefully planned so as to maximize its marketing potential. Standard sales presentations for telemarketing operations can be divided into seven parts—four steps of the sale itself and three related tasks:

1. Call Preparation

2. Step I: Opening

3. Step II: Fact Finding

4. Step III: Persuading

5. Step IV: Closing

6. Ending

7. Record Management

Each step of the call is linked to the next by a **lead-in**, which is a transitional question or comment to help the conversation flow smoothly. Not all calls go through all steps. Some go through only the first one or two, others move from Step I to Step III.

Call Preparation

The first and last of these—call preparation and record management—take place before and after the call, yet are an integral part of the call. They are part of planning and are treated as carefully as the actual dialog. The quality of your record management will affect the quality of your call preparation and the call itself.

Call preparation includes refreshing your memory as to what transpired on previous calls in order to be completely ready to make your current phone contact. To prepare for a call, a TSR:

- selects the person or company to be contacted;

- locates the records on that person or company—either a file folder, a file card, or computer data;

- reviews information from previous contacts;

- notes any follow-ups that were required and checks to see that they were handled;

- decides what product or service to present, basing this decision on the review;

- reviews the pronunciation of the person's name, if known, or is prepared to ask for that information;

- is thoroughly familiar with the product or service that will be discussed;

- has the first 100 words or so of dialog carefully prepared, because these are the words that will determine whether or not the prospect/customer continues listening.

Step I: Opening

The **opening** is in many ways the most important step since it determines whether you will be able to continue your conversation. The opening covers the first few sentences at the beginning of a call (inbound or outbound), and these sentences must be effective.

The opening is highly variable; its wording depends on the type of call being made or received—a first call to a new prospect, a pre-arranged call to a regular customer, an inbound call, or a call to a company where the TSR does not know the name of the person who will make the buying decision. The variations will occur in the sentences you say after you have identified yourself. There are six basic openings reflecting the call's intent:

1. Securing decision-maker's name, including the correct pronunciation.

2. Making first call to new prospects.

3. Working with the decision-maker's secretary.

4. Making call to periodic contacts.

5. Making call to regular customers.

6. Taking inbound call.

All openings share a basic characteristic, regardless of the type of call: you immediately identify yourself to whoever answers the phone. (You will read more about this essential step in Chapter 5.) Let's look at each type of opening.

Securing decision-maker's Name

This type of opening is used to learn the name and title of the person who will make the decision to buy, meet with a sales representative, or do whatever the call is about. The opening to secure the decision-maker's name is the simplest type of opening, and often the call will not proceed beyond it on the first try. Learning the name of the decision-maker can be the sole purpose of a call. It enables you to take further action, such as sending a letter letting the decision-maker know that you will be contacting him or her again, and what the call will be about.

Once you learn the person's name, use it when making the next call. Asking for a person by name and title increases the chances of being connected, as does a letter of introduction.

Often you will have the name of the person you are calling, but when you do not have a name, ask the person answering the phone for the name using a polite, conversational phrase that projects confident expectancy. He or she will usually be receptive to giving the information.

- *I'm calling for the head of purchasing. To whom will I be speaking, please?*

Be certain to secure the correct spelling and pronunciation, and record this information in your permanent records. Dale Carnegie says that a person's name is to him or her the most important sound in any language. When you hear your name pronounced correctly it produces a positive image in your mind; when it is pronounced incorrectly it produces a very negative image:

- "If this person (meaning the salesperson) can't even pronounce my name, he or she can't be very knowledgeable about the product/service either."

> **Openers to avoid when you are talking with people you don't know:**
>
> How are things?
>
> How goes it?
>
> How's the world treating you?
>
> What's going on today?
>
> What's new?
>
> What irons do you have in the fire today?
>
> What's the good word?
>
> What's up?
>
> How are you?
>
> What's new in your world?
>
> <u>NOTE</u>
>
> These openers *can* be used with people you visit with on a regular basis. When you know someone, you can genuinely care how they are or what is new. If you don't, these greetings have a note of insincerity.

That usually ends the hope of a sale. Yes—a person's name is that important. Pronouncing it correctly each time a contact is made is that critical!

To secure the correct pronunciation of the decision-maker's name from the secretary, the decision-maker personally, or someone else who answers the phone, open the conversation by saying something like this:

- *Hello, my name is _____ and I'm calling for (say the name as well as you can), please. Am I pronouncing the name correctly?*

Do not pause between sentences. If you are incorrect, the person answering the phone will give the correct pronunciation. This is the time to write it down *as it sounds* for a solid reminder of how it is pronounced.

- *If the secretary/other person identified him- or herself when answering the phone*, use the name in thanking that person for helping.

- *If the secretary/other person did not identify him- or herself when answering the phone*, ask for that person's name by using a transitional phrase: "By the way, what is your name, please?" After hearing the name, say, "Thank you, (name), for all your help."

This person's name is then also recorded in the permanent records. Whether it is a secretary or a spouse, he or she is part of a team with the decision-maker, and it is important to know and use the name correctly whenever you touch base.

To secure the correct spelling of the decision-maker's name, ask the secretary or the decision-maker.

If the secretary/other person tells you that the decision-maker is not there, follow this procedure. First ask when to call back; then use a transitional phrase to ask for the correct spelling:

- *Oh, by the way, what is the correct spelling of (decision-maker's) name?*

If you speak to the decision-maker directly, of course, you can ask him or her at the same time you verify the pronunciation.

New Prospects

This opening can be divided into four subsegments:

First—As always, identify yourself and your company.

- *Hello, I'm (name) with XYZ Company.*

Please note that the prospect's name is not used at this point.

Second—Give the purpose of the call. If some traditional marketing tool has been used prior to the call, you can mention it:

- *I'm calling about the letter we sent last week.*

Even if the prospect hasn't read it, this part of the opening serves to pique his or her curiosity, and helps move the call beyond the opening step.

In the rare event that no letter or advertisement has been used, simply identify the reason for the call:

- *I'm calling to share an idea with you about...*

You would briefly identify the product or service.

Third—Ask for the prospect's time. Think of telesales as a series of selling points that lead up to asking for the order–the actual sale. Asking for prospects' time is selling them on the *idea* of *giving* some time. This displays courtesy and respect and is effective because people appreciate consideration. This is an example of a *planned telephone dialog*.

A planned telephone dialog is like a good conversation, with each person having the opportunity to speak. Phrases encouraging questions and comments are part of a planned telephone dialog to guarantee an exchange of ideas. Always ask, "Am I reaching you at a good time?"

The hard-sell approach is to jump right into a presentation without asking for time. This causes a negative response, regardless of the reaction to the product/service itself.

If you sell the prospect/customer on the idea of giving you time, the rule of thumb is that the prospect/customer is prepared to give you about two minutes, unless you have been specific about the amount of time that you need.

If your prepared telephone dialog will take more than two minutes, the soft sell approach is always to send a note prior to the call letting the prospect/customer know its approximate length. Then, when the you ask for time in your prepared dialog, you mention again the amount of time that will be needed:

- *Hello, this is (name) with (company name). I am calling about the note I sent about our five-minute survey. Am I reaching you at a good time?*

If prospects/customers do not have time, you can make another mini-sale: selling them on the *idea* of talking again in the future. You give the prospect/customer *alternative* times to be called back, rather than simply asking when would be convenient. An example of the planned pair of alternatives that is always used would be:

- *Since that's the case, I won't take any more of your time today. Instead, may I give you a call later today or would sometime tomorrow be better?*

By using a pair of alternatives and this question, you can expect a positive response in which the prospect/customer chooses one or the other. When people are presented with specific alternatives they almost always choose one or the other. Simply asking for a convenient time to call back produces far fewer positive responses, because when people are presented with no specific choice, they most often choose *not to make any choice*, giving a "No, I'm not interested." response.

When a prospect/customer grants permission to call back, you have a wonderful opportunity to build trust and confidence. Many unprofessional TSRs do not call back when they promise, so when a professional TSR does indeed call back as promised, the prospect/customer begins to feel that this TSR will be there *after the sale* to provide quality service. This is one of the main reasons why it takes so many contacts before some decision-makers decide to buy: they want to make sure they will receive service after the sale.

Fourth—If the prospect has time to talk, give an initial benefit statement. An **initial benefit statement** is a brief description of the product/service and one of its most important characteristics. It is usually one sentence with enough information to interest the prospect. Before you give the initial benefit statement, however, repeat the reason for your call.

In a planned conversational dialog, it is important to give the prospect/customer many opportunities to respond. Planning, however, means that the exact location of the response is built into the dialog. You do not want a premature response at this point. Therefore, repeat the reason for your call in this fashion:

- *Thank you (name). As I mentioned, I'm calling about....*

Immediately follow this with a *third party influence* (see below) and an initial benefit statement. This is a valuable soft sell technique, used to avoid negative input from the prospect/customer at this point in the dialog. In an unplanned invitation for prospect/customer input at this (the wrong) part of the dialog, the TSR might ask if the prospect/customer received the letter that was sent. Often this results in a negative response, such as:

- *Yes, I did, and I'm not interested.*

The only recourse the TSR then has is to ask for an appointment to touch base in three months.

- Remember—telemarketing is the *planned* use of the telephone.

The **third party influence** can be anyone who has used and enjoyed the product/service you offer. It is a way of presenting the initial benefit statement in a soft sell manner, making it possible for the prospect/customer to agree to participate in the telephone dialog without feeling pressured to buy.

A third party influence is an individual in the case of a **referral**, which is a suggestion that the TSR call the person's friend, relative, or business associate about the product/service. This is often done in both business-to-business and business-to-consumer contacts. The name of the person giving the referral is the third party influence used in the *planned* telephone dialog. An example of an initial benefit statement using an individual for third party influence would be:

- *Pat Jones suggested I give you a call because he felt that you might want to hear about our (product/service), since you had mentioned that you were going to look into how a (product/service) would work in your office.*

A third party influence can be any *group* of people that use and enjoy the product/service being offered for consideration. This type of third party influence may be:

many people	many teachers
many customers	many lawyers
many families	many farmers

The TSR selects the appropriate group and might say, for instance:

- *Thank you. As I mentioned, I'm calling about our Universal Life Product. Many of our customers have felt relieved knowing that our life insurance not only gives them the advantages of flexible premiums; it provides ongoing protection for their family. With this in mind, may I please ask you a few questions about how this might work for you?*

An example of the hard-sell approach used all too often to present the initial benefit statement to prospects/customers is:

- *Thank you. As I mentioned, I'm calling about our Universal Life Product. It has flexible interest rates so you can take advantage of rates when they go up and it would give you protection for your family.*

The words *you* and *your* in the hard-sell approach create a feeling of pressure. They make the prospect/customer sense that the TSR *assumes* he or she will buy. In the hard-sell approach people are not asked for their permission to be questioned—the questions are just asked, causing more feelings of pressure. Prospects/customers become upset. They may use harsh words or hang up. This hard-sell approach gives the telemarketing industry a bad image.

Working With the Secretary

In business-to-business telemarketing, the decision-makers you want to reach, with the exception of some who have one-person businesses, will probably have secretaries. The decision-maker and the secretary are a team. Each secretary's main task is to save time for the person(s) for whom he or she works. This may include determining which phone calls are important and necessary and which ones are time wasters.

It is important that you project the confidence of a telemarketing professional and use the same soft sell approach when communicating with the secretary as you would with the decision-maker—that of respect, courtesy, friendliness, and helpfulness. When you do, the secretary will almost always respond with the same attitude.

The decision-maker and secretary are a team that TSRs always treat with courtesy.

It helps the secretary if TSRs send a note to the decision-maker to introduce themselves and to let the decision-maker know they will be calling and why. If the decision-maker doesn't want to receive the call, he or she will usually let the secretary know. This takes the guesswork out of the call for the secretary.

As you read earlier, most sales are made after the fourth or fifth contact. Therefore the TSR has many contacts with the secretary, trying to reach the decision-maker on one of these contacts. (Remember that each of the contacts made after the initial one is made with the decision-maker's permission.) Learning, recording, and courteously using the secretary's name help build a rapport and keep the lines of communication open.

As you read earlier, when a TSR projects confidence, whether it is with the secretary or the decision-maker, it is a sure sign of professionalism. Confidence begins with a positive attitude, which you will read about in Chapter 6.

Periodic Contacts

Once the initial contact has been made, openings for later calls are almost automatically provided by what transpired during the first call. Even if the initial contact only went as far as securing the decision-maker's name, the next call can begin with a reference to it. You have asked permission to call again in a few weeks or months, even if the prospect says "No" to a product/service. Times change, and the prospect may feel differently in the future. Maintaining regular contact shows genuine interest on your part and keeps the possibility of making a sale alive.

Each time you call back you go through a modified version of the opening step: identifying yourself and your company; identifying the purpose of the call; asking for the prospect's time; using third party influence; and giving an initial benefit statement.

Regular Customers

This opening is essentially the same as the previous one, except that you have already established a rapport with the customer, so that the tone is more casual, and friendly. This opening is used with regular customers and with prospects you have been contacting on a regular basis. It also includes initial contacts with prospects you know well. Even though you know the person, you immediately identify yourself. Making people guess your identity is not courteous because it is a waste of their time and may make them feel uncomfortable.

Inbound Calls

The primary consideration when opening an inbound call is always to determine why the prospect/customer has called, and to take care of that need immediately. There are, however, a few variations on the one basic theme.

In some cases, in order to provide prompt, efficient service, you need the prospect/customer's name immediately, and possibly an account number or some other identification code. In such a situation you would follow this basic pattern:

> TSR: (Company name), *this is* (name). *May I ask who's calling, please?*
>
> P/C: (Gives name)
>
> TSR: *Thank you for calling* (company name). *How can I help you?*

In other cases the caller's name is not required—at least not at first. In these situations you would use an opening without securing the caller's name.

A third variation on the inbound call opening involves the addition of an add-on sale lead-in. This requires discretion—you will not want to seem as though you are pushing something on the prospect before the prospect has stated fully his or her reason for making the call and has indicated satisfaction with your response.

This third variation is used only when a mass mailing generates a large number of inbound calls on the 800 number. In this situation, it is important that customers have only a minimal wait before a TSR takes their calls. The TSR uses this opening to save time in identifying the purpose of the call, but it doubles as an initiator of an add-on suggestion sale (see Chapter 3).

- *Thank you for calling (company), this is (name). Might you be calling in reference to our sale on (product/service)?*

If the person called for some other reason the answer will be "No, I'm calling about . . . ." The TSR takes care of the caller's needs; then uses a transitional phrase and makes an add-on suggestion:

- *By the way, although you weren't calling about our special on (product/service), would you like me to go over it for you?*

Moving On

The next step begins, as does each of the subsequent steps, with a lead-in question. A lead-in is a soft sell question to secure either a positive or a negative response. This response indicates what step of the sales process the prospect/customer is in. This takes the guesswork out of what the TSR is to do next. Lead-ins help the TSR move confidently from step to step. For instance:

If the response to the lead-in question is positive, the TSR knows that the prospect/customer has mentally moved into the next step and begins asking one of the three types of fact-finding questions.

If the response to the lead-in question is negative, the TSR knows that the prospect/customer has not moved into the next step, so the TSR remains in the same step and takes appropriate action.

Lead-In to Step II

If the response to this lead-in is negative, it means that the initial benefit statement has not stimulated enough interest for the prospect/customer to want to hear more, so the TSR ends the call by asking permission to call back at an appropriate time. The TSR records what step of the sale the prospect/customer was in, and the *plan* for the next phone contact— perhaps giving a different initial benefit statement or offering a different product/service.

Lead-In to Step III

A negative response to this step indicates that the TSR's first questions did not identify the wants and/or needs of the prospect/customer. The TSR then asks a few more questions if the prospect/customer seems receptive. If, however, the TSR senses that the prospect/customer is unreceptive, the TSR ends the phone contact in the same way as in the opening step.

Lead-In to Step IV

A negative response indicates that the first features and benefits the TSR gave about the product/service did not stimulate the prospect/customer's desire for what was being offered. So, if the prospect/customer seems receptive, the TSR gives a couple more features and benefits and asks another lead-in question. If, however, the prospect/customer seems unreceptive, the TSR ends the phone contact in the same way as in the opening step.

Conversational is Confident

Another reason the TSR feels confident in proceeding through the steps is that a lead-in serves a dual purpose. Besides taking the guesswork out of selling by providing indicators that let the TSR know exactly what to do next, the lead-in guarantees a non-pressure approach because the prospect/customer is asked for consent before the TSR moves on to the next step. This creates a comfortable atmosphere for both the prospect/customer and the TSR.

Step II: Fact Finding

Fact finding is the process of determining the prospect/customer's wants, needs, history, and current situation, in order to know which product/service is appropriate, and how it can best be presented. There are also other reasons for doing this.

Asking questions demonstrates interest. It allows you to become better acquainted with the prospect/customer, which builds rapport, aids in understanding when the prospect/customer has complaints or questions, and improves the chances of making a sale.

Questions allow the prospect/customer to do some of the talking. This builds trust and confidence. It maintains interest by keeping the prospect/customer actively involved and stimulates his or her thinking. Furthermore, when you listen, the prospect/customer is encouraged to listen to you. You will read more about listening and asking questions in Chapter 12.

Finally, questions help you maintain positive control of the conversation. They can be used to bring the prospect/customer back to the point, without seeming rude. Asking questions and really listening to the answers shows your sincere interest.

The most important reason, however, is to learn about the prospect/customer's wants and needs. Three types of questions should be asked in this step of the sale:

1. questions about *background and present situation*,

2. questions about *dissatisfaction, changes, problems,*

3. *trial-closing questions.*

Background and Present Situation

Background and present situation questions elicit essential facts about the prospect/customer's situation with the product or service that she or he currently owns or uses. They include questions on what product or service the prospect/customer currently owns or uses, how long it has been in use, what it is used for, the needs it fills and the demands made on it.

For example, if the service is a lawn care service, ask questions to determine how large the lawn is, and what fertilizer or watering it needs. Once you have such information, move to questions on dissatisfactions and changes.

Dissatisfaction and Problems

Asking questions about *dissatisfaction and problems* is the only time in the call in which negative subjects are discussed. Prospects/customers need to think about their dissatisfactions to determine what might improve the situation. With these questions, you find out what prospects/customers do not like about a product/service they use now, what problems they face conducting their operations, and what changes they may be considering. Only by asking prospects/customers what they consider to be wrong and what they may want to change, can you assist them.

Even when the prospect/customer has what is clearly a problem, however, do not use the word "problem," which brings to mind such things as spouse problems, children problems, money problems, health problems or car problems. Such negative thoughts distract the prospect/customer. Instead, use such terms as "dissatisfaction," "change" and "challenge" to stimulate your prospect/customer's thinking in a positive way.

Trial-closing questions

Trial-closing questions determine whether you have found your prospect/customer's main interest and help you test whether the prospect/customer is ready to move on to the next step of the sale. They are questions in non-pressure, conversational language, usually in hypothetical terms, that allow the prospect/customer to express feelings on various options without making a commitment.

If you were to....   *In your opinion....*
What do you feel...?   *Do you think...?*

During the fact finding you will form a mental picture of the prospect/customer's needs, making decisions about the particular product/service to meet those needs (for example, what model or level of service to recommend), and about how best to present it. But before moving into the persuading step, you should make sure you have in fact isolated the prospect/customer's interest. Ask a trial-closing question. Depending on the response, you might move to persuading, continue fact finding, end the call, or go directly to a closing question.

Step III: Persuading

Persuading refers to the step of the sale during which the *features* and *benefits* of the product/service are described. A **feature** is something the product/service is, has, does, provides or uses that makes it special and valuable. A **benefit** is what the feature gives the prospect/customer; like savings in time or money, ease of use, or increased capacity for work.

This step is all that many people think of when they think of telemarketing. As you have seen, however, persuading is not the whole story, and it requires preparation to be effective. A good TSR never leaps into persuading without establishing rapport and identifying the prospect/customer's wants or needs; otherwise, the only thing the prospect/customer is persuaded to do is to hang up.

The lead-in to this step begins with thanking the prospect/customer for answering your questions. You then refer to the material that has just been discussed, and relate it to what you are about to say: "Now, based on what we've just discussed, I'll go over how this product might work for you, if that's okay."

Once the transition has been made, three or four features and benefits are described:

- *This model operates at twice the speed of earlier versions [feature]. That means you save time and money [benefit].*

All too often TSRs rattle off features and benefits in a list, sounding like they are reading instead of sharing ideas in a conversational manner. The difference between sounding scripted and sounding conversational when giving features and benefits is the use of *softeners*. A **softener** is a phrase that ties each feature/benefit set together in a natural, casual, conversational way.

The following is an example of two features, connecting phrases, and benefits tied together in a conversational manner with the use of a softener. First read these two feature/benefit sets with the softener and observe how conversational it sounds. Then read them without the softener and see how it sounds as if you are reading a list. Always remember to use a softener between each feature/benefit set.

- *Our XYZ latex paint is guaranteed to last for five years—therefore, your walls will have the appearance you want year after year.*

- *What's remarkable is that... [softener]*

- *...speedy, effective power rollers can be used, so your whole interior can be painted and ready in one day.*

Then, ask what are called **feeling questions**. These are designed to find out how the prospect/customer is feeling about the product/service. For example, "How does this sound to you so far?" Feeling questions are another type of trial-closing question.

Depending on the response, these feeling questions can become lead-ins for the next step of the sale, the closing, or they can present an opportunity for more discussion of the product/service and the prospect/customer's needs. The persuading step can vary considerably in length, depending on the prospect/customer's response.

Step IV: Closing

The difference between a trial closing and a closing is that the former uses hypothetical phrases, whereas the latter is phrased in more definite terms. Because the finality of an actual closing is quite difficult to undo, prepare for it thoroughly. Use non-pressure techniques in your persuading and, when you think the prospect is interested, ask trial-closing questions to be sure it is time to ask for the order.

Trial-closing questions let you find out whether the prospect is ready for the closing, without forcing a decision before he or she is ready. A prospect/customer still in the thinking stage may say, "Not interested," rather than commit before being sure. If the response to a trial-closing question is positive, you can be reasonably sure the prospect/customer is really ready to buy.

A **closing question**, therefore, is one with which you definitively ask the prospect/customer for a decision to buy or lease the product/service, to arrange an appointment, or to buy into an idea.

By the time you have reached this stage, you will be fairly certain of where you stand. Using a confident tone and positive language, you simply put into words the feeling that has been developing throughout the previous steps. Ask for a decision:

- *Shall I go ahead and place an order for you today?*

Do Ask for Decision

The only way to make sales consistently is to ask prospects/customers for their decision. Many TSRs find asking closing questions uncomfortable. The main reason for their discomfort is their fear of a hard-sell approach that would upset the prospect/customer and, in turn, the TSR.

The soft sell approach creates a comfortable business atmosphere for both the prospect/customer and the TSR. In a planned dialog, giving the prospect/customer the opportunity to buy the product/service that you have been offering seems the only courteous thing to do after you have taken the person's time. The prospect/customer *expects* to be asked, so there is nothing to fear.

The following list summarizes the sales process and the several "mini-sales" the TSR makes throughout the steps of the sale.

- Opening Step: The TSR made an initial benefit statement about an important benefit of the product/service and then used a lead-in to ask if he or she could ask questions—*and the prospect/customer said yes*.

- Fact Finding Step: The TSR asked questions to find out the prospect/customer's wants and needs, followed by a lead-in to gain consent to give a few features and benefits—*and the prospect/customer said yes*.

- Persuading Step: The TSR fully described how the features and benefits of the product/service can meet the prospect/customer's needs, followed by a lead-in feeling question to find out the prospect/customer's feelings about the product/service—*and the response was positive*.

- The TSR asked questions to determine if the prospect/customer had any questions or objections about the product/service. The TSR answered these questions and objections and asked another feeling question to make sure that the prospect/customer was satisfied with the answers—*and the prospect/customer response was positive*.

- Closing Step: The TSR asked trial-closing questions to find out whether the prospect/customer is ready to make a decision in preparation for the closing—*and the response was positive*.

- The TSR asked a closing question to find out what decision the prospect/customer reached.

The prospect/customer will respond to this final question in one of three ways:

- *Yes*. The TSR takes care of filling the order.

- *I need more information*. The TSR handles the desired follow-up.

- *No, not now, I want to think it over*. This response does not mean that all is lost. The truth is quite the opposite.

As you will read in Chapter 6, most new business happens after the fifth "No." The reason is that some people are more cautious decision-makers than others. The facts show that only a small percentage of the population are quick decision-makers; most people need more time to think things through before they make up their minds.

Since the TSR knows that this week, next month, or next year circumstances may change, he or she asks for the opportunity to touch base by phone in an appropriate amount of time based on what has transpired during the phone contact. The prospects/customers who consent to receiving another call are added to the TSR's records and will receive a series of phone calls and direct mail pieces.

If you ask your closing question when the prospect/customer is ready, you have an excellent chance of making a sale. If you do not ask the closing question your chances of making a sale are less than ten percent, because only decisive, action-taking prospects are likely to place orders without being asked.

Be Cautious, Not Nervous

As a TSR, you need not be nervous about asking closing questions, only somewhat cautious. It is true that if you ask a solid, order-taking closing question too soon, you may receive a "no." And, after people say "no," they may not want to change what they say, for fear of appearing indecisive. That is why you precede your closing question with trial-closing questions. They are casual, low-key questions with which you determine whether the prospect is ready for an order-taking question.

All Phone Contacts End with Closing

Usually the term **closing** refers to making the sale: *closing* the deal. However, even asking permission to call the prospect back is a kind of selling—selling a future appointment to call back at a specific time. In this sense, every telemarketing call ends with a closing of some kind.

So even a call that does not end in a sale can use a closing question: "Since things have a way of changing in the business world, may I call to touch base with you in a few months?" Any procedure that sells the prospect/customer on an idea or particular plan can be thought of as a kind of closing.

Ending the Conversation

The actual completion of the call—saying "Good-bye" and hanging up the phone—is not part of the closing step. You do not simply hang up any more than you would just walk away from a face-to-face conversation without saying, "Good-bye." This is a matter of simple courtesy and is referred to in this text as **ending** the conversation. It can be compared to the complimentary close in a letter: "Sincerely," which is not part of the body of the letter.

Ending the call is a basic telephone skill that you should master no matter what kind of calls you handle. It involves making sure all business is complete and that the other person has nothing more to add. Always make sure the other person hangs up first. You will read more about such telephone skills in Chapter 5.

Telemarketing Records

A major benefit of telemarketing is its accountability. All professional telemarketing operations maintain detailed records of their day-to-day activities. This makes it possible for a company to evaluate daily progress, develop incentive programs, make projections, establish goals, and determine what revisions need to be made. The records provide information on the number of calls made, what happens on the calls and overall results. Every TSR must maintain call records. You will learn how in Chapter 7.

Vocabulary

80/20 rule	Initial Benefit Statement
Appointment Call	Job Description
Benefit	Lead-in
Bonus	Maintenance goals
Call Purpose	Opening
Closing	Persuading
Closing Question	Presentation
Cold Call	Product/Service Sales Call
Commission	Products
Customer Account Management	Prospect Base
	Prospect Development
Customer Base	Referral
Ending	Sales Call
Fact Finding	Service and Order Entry Call
Feature	Services
Feeling Question	Softener
Follow-up	Third Party Influence
Idea Call	Trial-closing question

Discussion Questions

1. What are the two major types of telemarketing prospect/customer? What kind of telemarketing is most widely accepted today? Why do you think this is so?

2. What are maintenance goals? Describe the two basic maintenance goals for any telemarketing operation. Explain why are they important.

3. What is prospect development and how does it work?

4. What are the three major types of customer account management? Explain how they differ.

5. What are the advantages of a Complete Account Management system?

6. What are the advantages of a Major/Marginal Account Management system?

7. What are the three types of telemarketing call that can be classified as sales calls? Explain how they differ.

8. Why are appointment calls useful?

9. Why are service calls useful? To whom might they be made?

10. Name and define the four steps of the sale.

11. Name the other three parts of a telesales call.

12. Describe the difference between a trial-closing and a closing question.

Activities

A. Setting up a Telemarketing Operation

Work with a small group on this activity. Pretend you are a company that is about to institute a telemarketing operation. Think about the size of the company (just a few employees, 50 to 100, over 100) and the product/service being sold. Which of the two prospect/customer types of telemarketing will you be dealing with? Each person in the group should pursue one of the two basic maintenance goals and describe some things he or she might do. Each person should describe which of the five basic types of telemarketing call he or she will use and for what purpose.

B. Matching Skills to System

Work with a partner from the same group. Discuss what you think are your strengths as TSRs. Decide whether you want to work independently under a Complete Account Management system, or together under a Major/Marginal system. If the latter, which of you will take the major accounts, which the marginal? Do not think of the marginal accounts as less important. Remember that managing marginal accounts requires marketing and sales skills, while handling major ones demands service skills. Marginal accounts also take longer to service because they require more calls to more customers.

- Telemarketing Strategies

- Primary and Secondary Call Purposes

- Matching Call Purposes to Career Paths

- Telemarketing Implementation Methods

- Human Resource Configurations

- Vocabulary

- Discussion Questions

- Activities

Chapter 3

Analyzing Strategies and Call Purposes

Upon completion of this chapter, you will be able to

(define the 11 major telemarketing strategies,

(distinguish between primary and secondary call purposes,

(identify the major call purposes in terms of the four career paths,

(describe the four methods for implementing the desired telemarketing strategy,

(describe four possible working arrangements for TSRs.

In this chapter, you will learn of the telemarketing industry's most widely used strategies and the steps that implement them. You will also read of the many call purposes that telemarketing can serve. A *call purpose*—or **telemarketing application**—is the identified reason for a call. Often a single call will have more than one purpose. Many calls will have a primary and a secondary purpose. You will also read of the methods of implementing the telemarketing effort and management's use of personnel to implement the operation.

Telemarketing Strategies

A **strategy** is an overall plan of action developed to accomplish clearly stated objectives. Although developing a strategy is a manager's responsibility, a TSR needs to be familiar with the main telemarketing strategies and the amount of planning required in order to follow the plan and ensure its success.

Eleven Strategies

In 1967, Eugene B. Kordahl and Donald Hoffman, two of the original members of the Phone Power/Telemarketing Professionals with the old Bell Telephone System, identified the first seven telemarketing strategies used in the telemarketing industry. Statistical data collected for the *Annual Guide to Telemarketing*, co-authored by Mr. Kordahl and Arnold L. Fishman, shows that the 11 telemarketing strategies listed below are the ones most used by companies today.

1. Sales programs to handle existing accounts.
2. Opening new accounts.
3. Suggestion-selling on incoming calls.
4. Qualification of prospect list.
5. Activating marginal, old, and forgotten accounts.
6. Introduction of new products and services.
7. Lead generation using direct-response 800 numbers.
8. Outbound contacts—business reply cards, coupons, and letters.
9. Follow up on direct-mail campaigns.

10. Full account management methods by territory, product, size.

11. Coordination of order entry and customer service procedures with marketing and telesales programs.

Strategy Development

To develop a telemarketing operation, management must:

1. Identify the objectives to accomplish and a strategy to reach these telesales or teleservice goals. Decide which telemarketing applications will be best to use. Project the investment and expected revenue.

   In small and medium sized companies, most management teams realize the importance of sharing the telemarketing strategy with their personnel early in the planning stages to dispel any fear that the company might plan a boiler room operation or replace outside salespersons with the telephone. This sharing ensures a higher level of cooperation.

2. Identify target markets (people or businesses to whom you intend to sell the product/service).

3. Compile or buy prospect lists.

4. Determine the primary call purpose. Then decide if a secondary purpose would enhance call effectiveness. (See below for more about primary and secondary call purposes.)

5. Select the method of implementation.

6. Select the personnel to implement the chosen method.

7. Select the telemarketing team players who will be involved on all levels.

8. Meet with this team and define all aspects of the strategy and each member's role.

> Small computer companies in the United States are rivalling giant, better-known companies with their flexibility, speed, and responsiveness to customer needs, according to an article in the January 1989 issue of *Inc.* magazine (Vol. 11, No. 1). Central to many of these companies' success is the use of telemarketing.
>
> Dell Computer Corporation, based in Texas, is one such company. Telemarketing gives Dell several advantages over its larger competitors. One is its ability to undersell the competition while retaining the quality of the product, by selling directly to the customer. Another is knowing the market. Over 1,000 phone calls a day give the company a strong sense of what people want, which enables it to respond quickly to new trends.
>
> A survey reported in *The New York Times* on January 8, 1989, found Dell service rated highly by business users of computers. Part of this success is no doubt due to the technical support offered over the phone.
>
> "A team of about 75 technicians deals daily with as many as 1,500 questions from customers," says the *Inc.* article. Design is also linked to customer response: if there are too many complaints about a part or product, the telemarketers go directly to the engineers, who alter the design as needed. The whole process takes a few days.
>
> "Direct marketing by phone is at the heart of Dell's success," *Inc.* reports. The company builds each customer's machine to order. "Dell's telemarketers take the customers' specs right off the phone. A number is assigned to each customer's request, specifying the kind of machine, the disk drive, memory size, and other components required. Each computer is then assembled and tested individually."
>
> *Inc.* credits telemarketing with giving small companies like Dell the ability to survive and flourish in a market that had been dominated by manufacturing giants. In the words of the opening caption, "Telemarketing created a $400-million beachhead in the PC industry."

9. Prepare the conversational telephone dialog, incorporate any desired traditional marketing tools, and prepare the record management system.

10. Train the telemarketing team.

11. Implement the strategy.

12. Monitor it.

13. Make any necessary revisions.

14. Conduct additional training where needed.

Primary and Secondary Call Purposes

Both inbound and outbound calls provide opportunities for a wide variety of telemarketing applications. Some applications are unique to the inbound call and some to the outbound; others can be used for both. Each telemarketing application is a purpose for a phone call—a primary purpose or a secondary one. Keep in mind that telemarketing applications and call purposes are interchangeable names. We will refer to them as call purposes.

Telemarketing is successful when management chooses a primary *purpose* and, most of the time, a secondary purpose, for each type of call, then chooses the best marketing tool for the purpose. There are a few call types that should not be used with a secondary purpose—for example, complaint follow-up calls. (See the section Matching Call Purposes to Career Paths that follows.) Marketing tools used in telemarketing, as in face-to-face sales, are:

- direct mail (flyers, brochures, envelope stuffers.)

- **media advertising** (advertising in radio, television, newspapers, magazines, and so forth.)

- **notes of introduction** (notes or letters to prospects/customers, letting them know that they will be receiving a call. Notes of introduction include an 800 number to call for those who do not want to receive the call.)

Primary Purpose

The **primary purpose** is the reason for the call. Having a

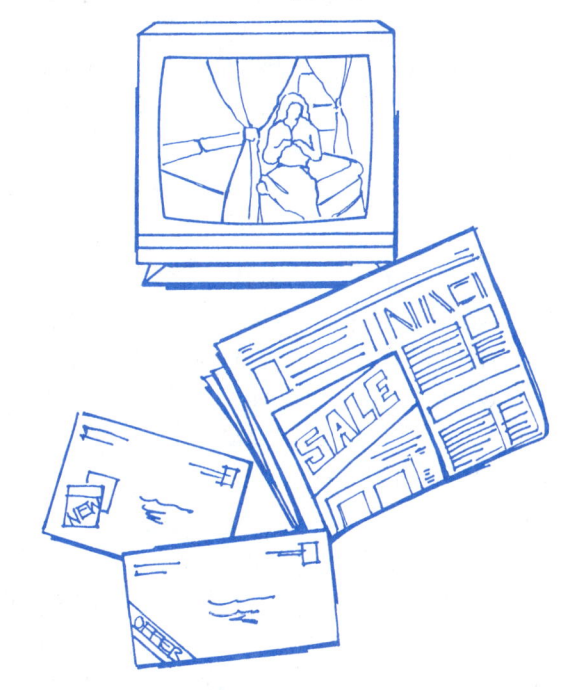

Direct method marketing tools include television, newspapers, direct mail.

specific, planned reason gives the call clear direction. The primary purpose can be any of the many telemarketing applications, like setting up an appointment or selling a product or service.

Secondary Purpose

The **secondary purpose** is to increase the sales potential of the call. It is simply another topic to discuss—a related product, a higher grade product, an upgrade or sale—once the primary purpose has been covered. Effective telemarketing operations train TSRs to prepare a secondary purpose to use with either outbound or inbound calls.

The secondary purpose could be almost any telemarketing application but it would be different from the primary purpose. It is used when the call goes well and the prospect/customer is receptive. (See the section on Indirect Method.) Secondary purposes can also be used on inbound calls. (See "Cross-Sell Suggestion" under "Matching Call Purposes to Career Paths," below.)

Matching Call Purposes to Career Paths

Following are descriptions of the major call purposes arranged according to the four telemarketing categories or career paths you learned of in Chapter 1: telesales, teleservice and teleorder (no sales), teleservice and teleorder (with sales), and marketing. The letters in parentheses after the purpose name indicate whether the calls are inbound, outbound, or both.

Visualize Your Career

As you read, visualize yourself using the various applications within each career path and begin thinking about which one you would enjoy the most. Keep these career paths in mind as you learn more about telemarketing so that you can develop a sense of what most appeals to you.

Pay particular attention to the differences among the career path applications because telemarketing is so new that many companies are actually unaware that there are four distinct career paths.

Understanding what is involved in these applications will help you to ask potential employers the right questions to find out if their available position is in a career path of your choice. Anyone who has a pleasant voice, good diction, is easily heard, and enjoys communicating with people can have a career in telemarketing. However, to have job satisfaction you will want to identify the career path that best fits you—sales oriented, service oriented, or a combination of both.

Telesales—Career Path One

Sales of Product or Service

© *Sales Follow-up (O)*—A call to customers a few days after they have purchased a product or service to see if it is working well, to help with instructions on use.

These calls may generate some complaints. Customers will, however, be talking to a company representative instead of complaining to others, and will appreciate that the company stands behind what it does. These calls satisfy customers and build long-lasting relationships.

© *Service Contract Sale or Renewal (O/I)*—Many products, such as home appliances, copiers, and computers, have **service contracts** that can be purchased along with them. The customer pays an annual fee for the contract, under which the company maintains and repairs the product. Customers do not always purchase this contract at the time of sale, and often appreciate another opportunity to buy the contract later.

© *Credit Application Solicitation (O)*—**Credit application solicitation calls** are made to encourage prospects/customers to apply for credit or charge cards. When customers have an opportunity to charge, they tend to increase their purchases. Customers regard such suggestion selling positively; it can be used as a secondary call purpose.

© *Referral Follow-up (O)*—A referral in traditional sales means that a salesperson receives the name of a potential customer from a third party, who gives permission to use his or her name. In telemarketing, **referral follow-up calls** work the same way.

Example: "Hello, I'm (TSR's name) with (Company) and I'm calling at the suggestion of (referrer's name). Am I reaching you at a good time?"

In this telemarketing application no suggestion selling is used on the initial call. The objective is to establish confidence and a rapport.

© *Reactivating Old Accounts (O)*—**Reactivating old accounts** is easier than starting new ones because the customer is familiar with the company's goods and services. The selection of old accounts to reactivate is based on their size and dollar volume.

The primary purpose of the call is to discover why the customer stopped doing business with the company and correct any dissatisfaction. There are many ways to reactivate an old account using telemarketing. Inviting former customers to be a part of a tele-information service seems to be the best. A **tele-information service** provides the former customer with regular updates on new products or services, improvements, changes, sales, special opportunities, and so on.

Old accounts can be reactivated by using any of the direct method call purposes that fit the company's operation. Indirect methods (suggestion selling) would be inappropriate on the call to reactivate an old account as the customer may feel pressured.

✆ *Updating Customer Records (O/I)*—This telemarketing application is another good way to reactivate old accounts. It is both a primary and a secondary call purpose.

TSRs are able to acquire additional information if they use a transitional phrase and open-ended questions that cannot be answered yes or no. For example: "Oh, by the way, we're updating our records, and we'd appreciate it if you had time to help us. For example, what changes have you made in your equipment since we last spoke?"

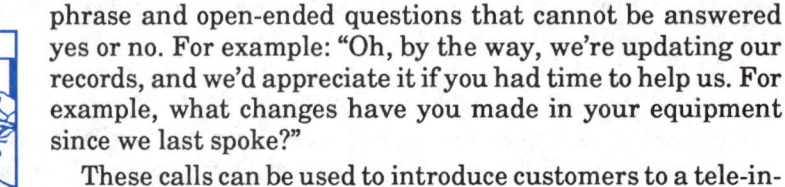

These calls can be used to introduce customers to a tele-information service. Any of the other indirect sales methods are also effective on these calls.

✆ *Updating Prospect Records (O/I)*—As its name suggests, this call purpose is similar to updating customer records, except the target group is people who have not yet become customers. Prospect record follow-up often takes a back seat because of lack of time, but it can be both a primary and a secondary call purpose to keep the prospect base growing.

Updating a prospect's records as a primary call purpose reestablishes contact. Open-ended questions work best. The calls can also be used with the other indirect sales methods and to introduce a tele-information service.

✆ *Lead Qualification Calls (O)*—TSRs make **lead qualification calls** to prospects that have been identified through traditional marketing methods. TSRs ask questions to ascertain interest level. Many people sign up or send in cards to be part of a drawing or for a free gift and have no real interest in the product or service. A lead qualification call saves valuable sales time.

✆ *New Product or Service Introduction (O/I)*—TSRs use the appropriate marketing tool and then make **new product or service introduction calls** to prospects in a targeted area. This is a well-received type of call—it lets interested people know of a product's availability.

✆ *Free Introductory Offer/Goods and Services (O/I)*—TSRs call to ask permission to send an item, such as a newspaper, free for a week, or to provide a one-time free service, such as lawn care. Such offers are usually made for ongoing purchases. TSRs make follow-up calls to answer questions and to see if the prospect/customer wants to purchase.

✆ Free Trial Offer/Returnable Merchandise (O/I)—A **free trial offer** is an excellent call purpose. A free trial offer gives prospects/customers time to try out a product and to think it over. TSRs make follow-up calls to answer questions and to ask for the order.

The difference between a free trial offer and a free introductory offer is that with a trial offer, if you do not want it, you return the merchandise. Since a service cannot be returned, it does not fit into this telemarketing purpose.

A variant is to *Offer an Item on Approval*, which differs from a free trial offer in that it lets the prospect look a product over without using it. For example, a hat, a suit, or pair of shoes could be tried on, not worn.

✆ Free Gift Offer (O)—This call offers a prospect a free gift for using a product or service, or for agreeing to an appointment for a demonstration or presentation. There is no obligation and the prospect keeps the gift whether he or she buys anything. The **free gift offer** is only as good as the quality of the gift and the legitimacy of the offer.

A follow-up call is made, with permission, to answer questions and to ask for the order. If the prospect does not purchase the product/service at this time, another follow-up call can be made later, again with permission, to answer further questions and again to try to make a sale.

✆ Feature Offer (O/I)—This call can be a quick money generator when used with a qualified prospect list. The purpose is to tell prospects about special sales or services. In effective telemarketing, TSRs constantly update lists of qualified prospects by keeping good records of those who love a special and those who are not likely to take advantage of the special. With their permission, TSRs call the qualified prospects on a regular basis. This works well as a secondary call purpose for inbound calls also.

The product or service on sale is known as a *loss leader* in retailing. (**Retail** stores are ones that sell directly to consumers, as opposed to those who sell in bulk to other stores). A **loss leader** is a product that is being sold at a low price, probably no more than cost, on which the store does not make money. The store hopes that this bargain will lure customers into making further purchases. Thus, a secondary purpose for this call is planned use of a suggestion selling option to increase the dollar volume of the call.

✆ Traffic Builder Calls (O/I)—**Traffic builder calls** are designed to increase the number of people who come to a place of business. These can be outbound calls made by the TSR, or inbound calls from the customer. If a company follows up its written invitation to attend its anniversary, open house, or sale, with an outbound call to invite the customer personally, traffic increases. The indirect method or suggestion selling also works well in traffic builder calls. When prospects/customers call customer service for a

positive reason, the TSR can easily extend a personal invitation to visit the business.

☏ *Introduction of a Tele-Information Service (O/I)*—This call purpose can fit any business or profession. This primary call purpose is to secure customers' permission to call them on a regular basis with information on product sales, tax laws, annual physical checkups, or whatever is appropriate.

☏ *Direct Response Call (I)*—Also referred to as a **consumer response call**, the **direct response call** is made by a prospect who has become interested through a direct marketing method. When the caller has completed her/his inbound call purpose, which is usually to place an order or seek information, the TSR can increase the volume of the sale (or possibly make one) by using one of the suggestion selling options. Many companies use this call-in as a source of leads to start a telemarketing outbound effort. They give the caller an overview of their tele-information service and ask if the prospect would like to be called periodically to receive information about new company products or services.

☏ *Catalog Sales (O/I)*—**Catalog sales calls** can be either outbound or inbound. Outbound calls are made to obtain permission to send a catalog and, subsequently, permission to call the prospect/customer on a regular basis. A catalog encourages inbound calls as well as acceptance of outbound calls.

Sale of the Appointment

☏ *Appointment Securing (Without Qualification) (O/I)*

Appointment securing without qualification means that a person called by a TSR or placing a call to a company is given an initial benefit statement and then asked if he or she wants to arrange a time to visit about the product/service offered.

This approach to appointment securing is used when products dealing with finances, such as insurance or stocks, are being offered to a new prospect. People view questions about financial information, from someone they do not know, especially over the phone, as an invasion of privacy, so no qualifying questions are used in the soft sell approach.

Talking with a customer using a catalog makes it easier to take orders.

© *Appointment Securing (With Qualification) (O/I)*—**Appointment securing with qualification** is used when the product is a personal possession, such as a home, automobile, or computer, or the service is something nonthreatening, like lawn care. In these cases, people are very open to answering qualifying questions over the phone, if their permssion has been asked. Therefore, prior to asking if an appointment can be arranged, a few qualifying questions are asked to see if the meeting would be appropriate.

Sale of the Idea
© *Fund Raising Calls (O/I)*—The **fund raising** telemarketing application is used extensively worldwide. Almost every organization, college, and church has fund raising campaigns that require telephone work. TV telethons have been a big business for years, especially in the health field. Public television and public radio stations regularly raise funds using this method.

Fund raising calls can be completely outbound calls in which TSRs or volunteers make calls to selected prospects and sell them on the idea of giving a donation. They can also be inbound calls encouraged by radio or television pleas.

© *Telecollection (O)*—**Telecollection calls** are made to keep accounts current. Planned, scheduled reminder calls made when an account is slightly overdue and the balance is small are easier for both the TSR and the person called. No selling is done on this call; the primary purpose is to sell the customer on the idea of working out a satisfactory payment arrangement.

© *Recruiting (O/I)*—A **recruiting call** addresses a targeted market. People in the targeted group are asked to buy the idea of joining an organization (such as a health club), becoming a member of the armed forces, or enrolling in college. Recruiting calls can have either one of two primary purposes:

1. to secure an appointment (the prospect agrees to tour a health club, visit a recruiting office, or meet with a group of students to discuss enrolling in a school);

2. to secure a *commitment* (have the prospect agree to join, enroll, volunteer).

Teleservice/Teleorder (Non-sales)—Career Path Two

© *Customer Service (O/I)*—More and more companies are realizing the importance of giving good service after the sale in order to retain their customer base and customer satisfaction. A customer service call can be an inbound call made by a customer to ask for information, make arrangements to have a product he or she purchased repaired, check on an order delivery or billing, make changes in a company service being used, or register a complaint. Because of the importance of handling complaints carefully, this is a seperate call purpose and is described later in this chapter.

An outbound customer service call is one made by a TSR in follow-up to something the customer wanted done or sent. Many companies want their customer service people to take care of the needs of the customer and not use suggestion selling. This is sometimes called **pure teleservice,** since it is a totally nonsales function.

☏ *Order Entry (O/I)*—An **order entry** call is an inbound call made by a customer to place an order for a product or service. Just as with the customer service call, there is no suggestion selling done. Order entry can also take place during outbound calls made for some other purpose.

☏ *Complaint (I)*—A customer calls in with a complaint. The TSR takes immediate positive action to correct the situation. No selling is attempted.

☏ *Complaint Follow-up (O)*—A few days after the initial complaint call, the TSR makes this outbound customer service call to make certain that the situation has been resolved satisfactorily. This call is an extra measure of service that helps rebuild customer trust and confidence. The only purpose of this call is to settle the issue and retain a satisfied customer. No selling is done.

Teleservice/Teleorder (With Sales)—Career Path Three
Suggestion Selling (SS)

☏ *Customer Service (O/I) and Order Entry*—Unlike such calls in career path two, these in career path three include suggestion selling (SS). The TSR first makes certain that all the needs of the customer are taken care of. Then, to increase or generate revenue, if the tone of the call is positive, the TSR uses a soft sell transitional phrase, such as, "Oh, by the way," to move into suggestion selling activity, such as the following.

☏ *Tie-In Suggestion (O/I)*—To implement the **tie-in suggestion,** TSRs use a transitional phrase to change the subject from the product/service the customer has purchased to an accessory that ties in with the purchase. Example: after a customer has ordered a pen and pencil set, the TSR suggests some writing paper. This is suggestion selling and is a secondary purpose.

☏ *Add-On Suggestion (O/I)*—The **add-on suggestion** is similar to the tie-in suggestion. The key difference between them is that the add-on can be something totally unrelated to the original sale.

☏ *Up-Sell Suggestions (I)*—**Up-sell suggestions** become the secondary call purpose when a prospect/customer calls regarding a specific product or service, and TSRs, after courteously giving the information, offer alternate choices of higher grades and describe their features and benefits.

☏ *Cross-Sell Suggestion (I)*—A TSR uses **cross-sell suggestion** when a prospect/customer initiates a call but does not purchase the call-in interest item. At that point, the TSR suggests an alternate item that is unrelated to the original item.

Marketing—Career Path Four

☏ *Market Research (O)*—Remember the difference between marketing and sales. Market research is usually the first step in marketing. *Market research calls* are made to determine the marketing possibilities of a product or service.

Most market research is done by companies that specialize in this service, and it is wise to use such a firm. Making the calls is relatively simple, but developing a comprehensive questionnaire and analyzing the data requires a specialized knowledge and skill.

☏ *Survey Call (Lead Generation) (O)*—Many companies use **survey calls** to collect data on which to base marketing strategies or product/service offers. A company's credibility rests on the honesty of such survey calls. Using a fake survey as an opening to selling a product is unethical.

Telemarketing Implementation Methods

After the primary and secondary purposes of a call have been established, a company determines the implementation method that best fits its strategy. Four major methods can be used in both inbound and outbound calls in various combinations.

Direct Method

In the **direct method**, used with the primary purpose of the calls, the company uses marketing tools and techniques to generate leads, to heighten the prospect/customer's acceptance level for outbound calls, and to encourage prospects/customers to make inbound calls.

Outbound Direct Method

The **outbound direct method** uses a traditional marketing tool to inform prospects of a proposed call and its primary purpose. The note of introduction or the direct mail piece always lists an 800 number to give the prospect the opportunity to call and decline to receive a call. This technique is a great lead qualifier, time saver, and rejection reducer. The TSRs call only people predisposed to receive a call.

Inbound Direct Method

The **inbound direct method** is designed to generate inbound calls. It also uses a traditional marketing tool, such as direct mail or media advertising. The marketing message is intended to encourage prospects/customers to call to place an order for a product/service or to seek information.

Companies receive many inbound calls during their regular business day. People call to make complaints, seek information, ask for service, or to place orders. These calls, which are not made in response to a specific marketing effort, are normal business phone activity and not part of the inbound direct method, although they are part of telemarketing.

Indirect Method

Indirect method, or **suggestion selling**, can be used, after the caller's needs are taken care of, for the secondary purpose of calls. Suggestion selling means to suggest another product, service or idea to the customer in addition to the specific one that was the reason for the call.

The objective is to increase sales dollar volume and to stimulate interest in a product/service so as to develop the purpose for the next call—and an ongoing telephone relationship with the prospect/customer. The indirect method can be used with either outbound or inbound calls.

Outbound Indirect Method

When TSRs complete the primary purpose of a call, they use a transitional phrase, such as "Oh, by the way," as a bridge to the planned secondary purpose of the call. The phrase fits easily into the conversation. Some secondary purposes might be to inform the prospect/customer about a new product, or to call attention to a related product or service.

Inbound Indirect Method

When TSRs have taken care of the caller's purpose for the inbound call, they use a natural transitional phrase to introduce the planned secondary purpose. Suggestion selling on inbound calls

Strategies and Call Purposes

> Partly because there are so many different call possibilities in telemarketing, planning is an important part of telemarketing. Planned aspects of the telemarketing process are:
>
> *Selecting specific telemarketing applications* (the various things a call can be used for—making appointments, introducing a product, and so on).
>
> *Identifying target markets* (the group of people or businesses, identified by some common theme, to whom you intend to sell the product/service).
>
> *Compiling or buying prospect lists.*
>
> *Determining the call's objective* (what the call is to accomplish) and the steps to reach that objective, including developing a sales presentation and creating a script. (You will read about scripts in Chapter 4.)

requires planning and preparation because TSRs never know the caller's purpose ahead of time.

The telemarketing manager usually helps prepare one or two options, such as a product-of-the-month sale or new product information, and instructs the TSRs on how to select the one appropriate for each inbound call.

This kind of planning makes a customer service call, which is a normal business phone activity, a revenue generating telemarketing application.

Human Resource Configurations

Different telemarketing operations use their personnel in different ways. The way they organize the TSRs' activities is called a **human resources configuration**. The point of any human resources configuration is to establish the most productive match of job responsibilities with skills and interests. Some people are very effective on the telephone, serving customers or taking orders, and less effective and even uninterested in face-to-face selling, while the opposite will be true of others. Some people may enjoy both selling on the phone and making face-to-face contact with prospects/customers.

Telemarketing operations, especially large ones, try to be aware of these differences and set up job assignments acccordingly. The sections below describe four possible working arrangements for

TSRs. When management selects the appropriate configuration for the strategy, it is called **human resource management**.

Inside Only

TSRs work in-house, with no outside contact with prospects/customers. All TSRs make planned outbound calls and receive inbound calls, or some TSRs make outbound calls while others receive inbound calls.

Inside/Outside—One Person

An outside sales representative (OSR) does some telemarketing and some outside sales calls. Two examples:

- A sales representative, using a system of planned phone calls, secures appointments with prospects/customers and then goes out on these appointments to make the sale.

- A sales representative calls on customers in person and arranges to service their accounts twice each month in person and twice by phone.

Telemate System

In some operations, TSRs form two-person teams to generate and service accounts. This is known as a **telemate system**. Teams can be set up to take advantage of each member's strengths and to minimize weaknesses. The team receives credit for the sale, and smart companies arrange shared bonuses or commissions.

Inside Only Sales Team

Both members of the team work in-house. One TSR calls on major customer accounts exclusively (the top 20 percent), and one TSR calls exclusively on marginal accounts (the other 80 percent). When a marginal account is built into a major account, based on dollar volume, the major account TSR takes it over. In exchange, two or three major accounts that border on marginal status and have the same combined dollar volume as the new major account go to the marginal account TSR for rebuilding.

Both telemates share bonuses or commissions on exchanged accounts. If this is not done, marginal account TSRs have little incentive to build accounts that they will lose with no financial gain. Even though there has been an exchange of equal dollar volume, it takes longer to sell and service three accounts than it does one.

Inside/Outside Sales Team

One TSR and OSR share the same prospects/customers. Variations on this telemate system include:

- A TSR secures the appointment for the OSR, who makes the face-to-face contact. Once the initial appointment has been made, the OSR makes all subsequent contact.

- The OSR works with prospects/customers to establish a comfortable ratio of phone and face-to-face contacts. Then TSR calls the customers and starts building a rapport with them. Commissions, bonuses, and credit are shared.

- The OSR has the major accounts and the inside TSR builds the marginal accounts.

Vocabulary

"(CP)" stands for "Call Purpose."

- Add-on Suggestion (CP)
- Appointment securing
  - with qualification (CP)
  - without qualification (CP)
- Catalog Sales Call (CP)
- Consumer Response Call (CP)
- Credit Application
  - Solicitation Call (CP)
- Cross-sell Suggestion (CP)
- Direct Method
- Direct Response Call (CP)
- Free Trial Offer (CP)
- Free Gift Offer (CP)
- Fund Raising (CP)
- Human Resources
  - Configuration
- Human Resource
  - Management
- Inbound Direct Method
- Indirect Method
- Lead Qualification Call (CP)
- Loss Leader
- Media Advertising
- New Product/Service
  - Introduction Call (CP)
- Note of Introduction
- Order Entry
- Outbound Direct Method
- Primary Purpose
- Pure Teleservice
- Reactivating Old Accounts (CP)
- Recruiting Call (CP)
- Referral Follow-up Call (CP)
- Retail
- Secondary Purpose
- Service Contract
- Strategy
- Suggestion Selling
- Survey Call (CP)
- Tele-information Service (CP)
- Telecollection Call (CP)
- Telemarketing Application
- Telemate System
- Tie-in Suggestion (CP)
- Traffic Builder Call (CP)
- Up-sell Suggestion (CP)

Discussion Questions

1. Define "telemarketing strategies."

2. How do the primary and the secondary purpose of a call differ?

3. Why is it important to have both a primary purpose and a secondary purpose for most types of calls?

4. Describe at least four call purposes that would come under Career Path One—Telesales.

5. What is the direct method? Describe the two kinds of direct method.

6. Are all inbound calls part of the inbound direct method? Why or why not?

7. Describe suggestion selling. What is another name for it? Identify some benefits of using suggestion selling, besides increasing sales dollar volume.

8. How is suggestion selling implemented during inbound calls?

9. What are four working arrangements for TSRs? Why are there different arrangements instead of one which is best in every case?

10. How do inside/inside telemate teams divide accounts? Explain why it is important they share commissions.

Activities

Work with the same group you were in in Chapter 2 and use the company description you drew up then.

A. Selecting Telemarketing Strategies

From the list of 11 strategies, select three or four appropriate for your product/service. Pick at least one each for selling, marketing, and servicing. For each strategy, describe the primary purpose of the call to be made. Select a secondary purpose for those calls that can use one. Be sure to distinguish between primary and secondary purposes.

B. Selecting an Implementation Method

Decide which implementation method best fits your company: outbound or inbound direct calls (indirect method is used with secondary purposes only). Determine the traditional marketing tools you will use. For example: a company that sells personal computers uses media advertising to generate inbound calls. Primary call purposes are order taking/information giving—inbound; customer retention—outbound; customer service/complaint—inbound, and telecollection—outbound. Secondary purposes can be added for the first two but not the second two primary purposes. Any of the suggestion selling purposes would be appropriate.

Knowing Your Company

Learning Scripts and Prompters

Preparing Prompters

Sample Script: Market Survey

Vocabulary

Discussion Questions

Activities

Chapter 4

Using Scripts and Prompters

Upon completion of this chapter, you will be able to

- Explain the difference between *scripts* and *prompters*,
- recognize the importance of knowing the company, its products and services,
- develop a method for memorizing scripts and product information,
- prepare a simple prompter.

"Telemarketing is the *planned* use of the telephone in conjunction with traditional marketing methods and techniques," and as part of this planned use, TSRs often follow an outline of the presentation, called a *prompter*, or use a script. In this chapter you will learn what a script is and how it differs from a prompter. You will also learn that to use either effectively, you must know your company and the product or services it offers.

A **script** is a written record of exactly what to say—questions to ask, suggestions to make, and so on. It is to be followed word for word.

Market research firms that depend on the validity of the data collected require that the same questions be asked each person using the same wording. Therefore they often use scripts. (A sample script is given at the end of this chapter.) Financial firms, insurance companies, and brokerage houses also use scripts. Another time when a script is used is when a telemarketing service bureau is taking inbound calls in response to an ad or mailing. A short script is used to save TSRs' time. Thus people calling in are not left on hold and their needs are taken care of quickly.

A **prompter** is in written form, but it is not to be read word for word. Rather, it serves to remind you (prompt you) of the points to be made in your own comfortable language. (See page 65 for a sample prompter.)

A major value of writing down what you want to say is that it ensures that you cover all of the important information. Having the words in front of you frees you from the need to concentrate on remembering everything that you need to say so that you can concentrate on *how* you are saying the words—how you sound. Good scripts and prompters include alternate language to cover different responses from the prospect.

In most telemarketing operations you will use an already prepared prompter or prepare one yourself. Remember the difference between a prompter and a script. A script is something you read word for word, because the exact phrasing is crucial. A prompter gives you key words and concepts, but you use your own words when talking on the phone. Generally you will be using a prompter and not a script as a telemarketer.

Knowing Your Company

The more you know of your company and what it offers, the easier it is for you to project feelings of interest and excitement as you talk to the prospect. It is difficult to use a prompter, or even a script, on subjects you know little about. Also, you would be unable to provide any answers beyond what is on the prompter, which would be limiting.

Good actors not only memorize their scripts, they also research the role they must play. They find out all they can about it even if

This is a sample telephone dialog prompter for a traffic builder call that a real estate company might use to encourage visitors to an open house. A letter has been sent inviting prospects to the open house and letting them know they will be receiving this reminder call. (Note all the built-in interaction.)

1. *Hello, Mrs. George Jones? I'm (give name) with Top Sell Real Estate. I'm calling about the open house we wrote you about. Am I reaching you at a good time?*

[If YES go to #3. If NO go to #2.]

2. *Since that's the case, I won't take any more of your time now, instead may I give you a call later or sometime tomorrow?*

[Write Time_____] [Go to #6]

3. *Great. We find people enjoy having the chance to see other homes to keep abreast of values, as well as to get ideas for increasing the value of their property. The open house is 10 a.m. to 4 p.m. Sunday. Do you think you'll be able to visit, Mrs. Jones?*

[If YES go to #5. If NO go to #4.]

4. *I'm sorry you can't make it. We're also having open house on Wednesday at 7 p.m. Would that be a better time for you?*

[If YES go to #5. If NO go to #7.]

5. *Wonderful! If you have interested friends, please feel free to bring them along. By the way, do you know anyone who might appreciate hearing about this open house?* [Go to #8.]

[Write names, addresses, telephone numbers. Say thank you.]

6. *Thank you, Mrs. Jones. I'll call you at* (time). *Goodbye now.*

7. *Yes, the timing isn't always right. Since things change, may I give you a call from time to time to keep you informed of listings in your area? Thank you, Mrs. Jones. Goodbye.*

8. *If it's okay with you, we'll call from time to time to keep you informed of listings in your area. Thank you, Mrs. Jones. Enjoy the open house. Goodbye.*

[Wait to hear other person hang up before hanging up.]

they know they will be reciting a script word for word. Good actors are aware that the more they know about the character they are playing, the more feeling and meaning they can put into the scripted words they say.

Good TSRs, whose job description requires the use of scripts, take the same approach. This is true whether their company is selling equipment to dentists or homeowners insurance or conducting a market survey. The greater their depth of knowledge the more effective their delivery.

You may work for a company that sells a variety of products or services, which makes it impossible for you to use the same approach on each call. In such situations, prepared scripts and even prompters are of limited use. In these situations, you would develop a thorough knowledge of the product, procedures, and services before you begin making calls so that you can answer all questions clearly and confidently. Keeping up with your company takes a least one hour a week to learn and to refresh your store of information. With this knowledge you can carry on effective sales conversations. If your company does not have a prepared prompter, you can write one of your own.

Learning Scripts and Prompters

The whole learning and recall process works best when the information you are learning is embedded in some kind of systematic framework. Say, for example, that you have seen a movie several times. The story line and other details—characters' faces, the setting, voices, other sounds—are vivid and easy to recall.

When you tell someone else about the movie, you are excited, you have fun doing it, you feel confident because you know what you are going to say and that it is going to be clearly understood by the listener.

The same thing is true when you want to recall information about the product or service. One way to do this is to imagine yourself using the product/service. Make up a "story" about how you would use it. It does not have to be at all complicated. On the contrary, keep it simple. Just give it a clear movement from beginning to end. Include as much information as you can about the product/service.

You learn more, and learning is easier, when you are relaxed. When you are relaxed, your brain functions more effectively. You no doubt have had the experience of performing poorly when you were tense or under pressure. Tension, with accompanying poor performance, can occur when you have a negative attitude. Professional TSRs practice techniques to help them relax and enhance their enjoyment of learning new material as well as making calls. See the box on this page for a simple relaxing routine to follow.

Scripts

To learn a script you are to say word for word, record on tape the script and other material to be learned and listen to it repeatedly in a relaxed frame of mind for several days. Doing this allows your brain to soak up the words like a sponge, and they go directly into your subconscious mind as speech, rather than as a written script.

As you are absorbing the material, your brain is connecting and recalling related information you have already stored away. The script and information about the product/service are now linked in your mind with a whole complex of related information, so that as you use the script, you will be able to select an appropriate response to any given question from the prospect/customer. This whole process of association and recall takes place in a split second.

A positive attitude is an important asset in using scripts and prompters. You will learn techniques for developing a positive attitude, which will help you deliver scripts in a natural, conversational manner, in Chapter 6.

Prompters

Before recording and listening to the tape, read the prompter for its meaning rather than its words. Think of new words to express the same idea. Write a prompter in your own words. Practice using

---

You absorb information more readily when your body is relaxed. The following exercise will help you to relax so that you can learn new material quickly and easily. It can be performed sitting in a comfortable chair that provides good back support.

- ✓ Tense your foot muscles. Hold to the count of five (count "One and two and three," etc.), then relax the muscles.
- ✓ Tense your leg muscles. Hold to the count of five, then relax.
- ✓ Tense your stomach muscles, count five, and relax.
- ✓ Repeat the procedure for your chest, arm, and neck muscles.

your words. Then go back to the original and read it aloud, concentrating on the points you covered in your version. Go over any other information you have about the product/service. Make note of the features you find most attractive, then look at the original prompter and read it aloud, using your voice to highlight the aspects you found appealing. Think of what the dialog is about, as well as the words.

By doing this you make the words *mean* something to you, which they do not do when they are just a collection of words someone has prepared. You remember things that are connected in your

---

You can improve your memory. All it takes is a little effort, some practice, and, yes, a positive attitude. Studies have shown that you can remember more when you tell yourself that you can. Begin with that positive attitude and use these simple tips to improve your memory when learning a script or about your company and its products or services.

- ✓ *Concentrate.* When you read your script or hear about your company pay close attention. The reason many people do not remember is that they never really heard or saw the material in the first place because they were not paying attention.

- ✓ *Take notes.* The act of writing something down increases the chances of your remembering it.

- ✓ *Shut out distractions.* Eliminate clutter—mind and physical clutter. Focus on one thing at a time. Give yourself time, especially when trying to remember information about several different products or services. Learn one thing, then take a break to let your mind absorb it before starting to learn something different.

Remembering names is particularly important for TSRs. Here are some tips for remembering names you hear for the first time on inbound calls. (On outbound calls you will have the name in front of you and will say it immediately to make sure you have it right.)

- ✓ Listen carefully when you first hear the name.

- ✓ Repeat the name immediately. For example, "Thank you for calling, Jan Wright, how can I help you."

- ✓ Use the name as often as naturally possible. Even if you do not say it aloud, repeat it often to yourself.

- ✓ Associate the name with a tone of voice or manner of speaking.

mind to other facts more easily than you remember unrelated bits. Much of your meaning is conveyed by the sound of your voice. If the words mean nothing to you, your voice sounds as though you are just mouthing nonsense.

Preparing Prompters

Sometimes you may be given the opportunity to prepare a telephone dialog prompter yourself, based on what you know about a product/service. When you prepare a prompter you need to consider people's rate of comprehension. In this regard, sentence length is important. Sentence length will affect your presentation and whether you hold the interest of the prospect/customer.

For practical purposes, you can think of comprehension as occurring at three levels—the level of the individual word, of a single sentence, and of groups of sentences about a single topic. The length of your sentences will play a part in how people understand your message at the second two levels—sentence and thought comprehension.

Here are some guidelines for planning and organizing scripts and presentations:

People use different techniques to help them to remember. There are several devices people have used successfully over the years. Associating things to remember with places in a city as described in the text is one such device. Another common one is making up rhymes. Rhyme in poetry probably began as an aid to memory of this sort. A well-known example of a rhyming memory aid for poor spellers is:

> *I* before *e*, except after *c*
> Or sounding like *way*
> As in *neighbor* or *weigh*.

A rhyme for remembering the number of days in a month is:

> Thirty days has September,
> April, June, and November.
> All the rest hold 31
> Except for February's sum,
> Which is but 28 so fine,
> Til leap year gives it 29.

Forming words and sentences is another memory device. For example, we remember the notes on the scale easier when we relate those in the spaces—F A C E—to the word *face*, and those on the lines—E G B D F—into the sentence: Every Good Boy Does Fine.

---

1. Approximately 120 words will make up a *thought* of several sentences.

2. A *short* sentence has 8 words or less.

3. An *average* sentence contains 15 to 20 words.

4. A *long* sentence is 21 words and over.

5. People understand best when thoughts are put into sentences of 15 to 20 words.

Keeping the Prospect/Customer's Attention

Comprehension and attention span go hand-in-hand. **Attention span** refers to the length of time a person can concentrate on what is being said. No matter how clearly you speak, or how well you choose your words, if the person's attention is lost, your message is just a lot of noise falling on uncomprehending ears.

People's attention is sustained when they have the opportunity to make comments, ask questions, and share ideas at the completion of each thought. This is what produces a *conversational* dialog rather than a sermon in which one person talks and the other person listens.

People's attention span is also affected by the way in which the length of sentences is varied. It is important to vary the lengths:

- a few long ones—20 words and over
- a few short ones—6-8 words
- the majority of moderate length—15 to 20 words

Varying sentence lengths gives speech a melodic rhythm. Without this variety of sentence length, speech becomes dull, bland, and monotonous—and the listener's attention is lost. Some sales conversations may need to be rather long, because of the nature of the product/service. This is perfectly acceptable if features and benefits are given in clusters of three or four sentences, with a prospect/customer response in between.

Incomplete Is Okay

Although a *thought* has been defined here as a group of 120 words, in several sentences, it is important to note that people do not speak *only in complete thoughts and complete sentences.*

Phrases—parts of sentences—are natural in conversation. That is one big difference between the spoken and the written word. Complete sentences are a requirement of most written English. Conversely, if you were to *speak* only in complete sentences you would sound rigid, precise, and stilted; your speech would lose its natural, conversational quality. The listener would get the feeling that you were holding a microphone and giving a prepared speech.

The same holds true when it comes to thoughts. For example, a sales conversation would not consist of two people taking turns exchanging 120-word thoughts. Instead, it would be a combination of three or four complete thoughts laced with questions, comments, quick ideas, subject changes, interruptions, etc.

Practice Varying Sentences

In practicing your presentation, concentrate on using different sentence lengths, breaking up long strings of words, and employing conversational phrases. You may not get the features you want at first. Practice your presentation several times to get one that will keep the attention of the prospect/customer.

Sample Script: Market Survey

Hello, (name)? *I'm* (your name). *I'm a student at* (school/college). *I'm calling about our community educational needs survey. Do you have a few minutes?*

(Prospect/customer says Yes.)

Thanks, (name). *As I mentioned, we're doing an educational needs survey of people in our area and would value your input. May I ask you a few questions?*

Thank you. Have you heard about our programs for adults? Where did you get the information? From newspapers? Radio? Television? Has anyone that you know attended any of our programs? Which ones? Do you know of anyone planning to further his or her education? In what field?

(School) *is offering several courses this coming semester, in different fields. Were you aware we have evening, daytime, and weekend programs. To develop a better awareness in the community of the programs* (School) *offers, we'd appreciate the opportunity of sending you one of our information packets. Would that be okay?*

Thank you for taking the time to answer my questions. As I mentioned, we want to determine what programs people in our community are looking for. We plan to add to the programs we already have, and I'd be glad to call you when the expanded schedule is ready if you'd like.

Vocabulary

Attention span
Prompter
Script

Discussion Questions

1. What is the difference between a prompter and a script? How does either help with calling?

2. Why is it important to learn the prompter or script and to learn about the product before calls are started?

3. Cite three steps to improve your memory. Remembering names is particularly important; name three techniques for remembering them.

4. How does having a framework for the information aid the memory? How does it help improve delivery?

5. How does sentence length affect the listener's attention span? Why is it important to vary sentence length in a prepared telephone dialog? What else can be done to help keep attention?

Activities

Use these activities to practice using prompters and scripts. They can be carried out with a partner in the classroom, or alone at home.

A. Developing Your Own Prompter

This activity will give you practice developing a prompter—an outline of key words and ideas to follow during a call.

Think of a product with which you are familiar. It can be one from the company you devised in the activities for Chapter 2, or some other product you feel comfortable with. Think about the qualities you appreciate in this product—how it helps you, what you enjoy about using or having it, reasons you might recommend it to a friend or coworker. If you are working with a partner, brainstorm together to come up with as many of these qualities as you can. Every time you think of a quality you want to share, write it down. Write down any descriptive words you or your partner use.

Think of a friend who could use this product but does not know about it. What would you ask this person about his or her current situation to find out whether the product would be appropriate? Make a note of the questions you would ask. Relate them to your knowledge of the product: does your friend need what the product has to offer? How might it help him or her?

Think about how you would present this product to a new acquaintance. Refer to the steps of the sale described in Chapter 2. Put together an outline following these steps. Pick a descriptive word or two from your list to use in an initial benefit statement. Use the questions you have devised for the fact-finding step of the sale. Make a note of the features and benefits you have listed to use during Step III, Persuading.

B. Using the Prompter

Now practice using this prompter in a telephone dialog (it is best to have a partner who can play the other person). You have the information you want to convey, but are not held to a rigid delivery. You can use your own comfortable language. Tape record the conversation, and analyze your sentences. Do they all stick to the same length, or is there an interesting variety? Practice varying the length of your sentences so as to hold the other person's interest.

C. Reading and Memorizing Scripts

Turn to the sample script on page 71. Turn on your tape recorder and sight-read the script. (Sight-read means to read it aloud without first going over it.) Listen to how you sound. Now go over the script again and think about how you can read it more effectively. Tape it again. Did you sound more natural? Listen and repeat the script until you can read it in a natural voice, word for word, without actually reading it.

Unit II
SKILLS + ATTITUDE

Chapter 5—Developing Service-Oriented Skills

Chapter 6—Developing a Positive Attitude

Chapter 7—Keeping Records

Effective Use of
Telephone Equipment

Procedure for All Calls

Procedure for Inbound Calls

Procedure for Outbound Calls

Vocabulary

Discussion Questions

Activities

Chapter 5

Developing Service-Oriented Skills

Upon completion of this chapter, you will be able to

- use telephone equipment effectively,

- develop a procedure for all calls that will project a service-oriented approach,

- employ four major skills for handling incoming calls,

- use eight techniques for improving outgoing calls.

In this chapter you will learn some simple steps to carry on a telemarketing conversation effectively and pleasantly. The focus here is on mechanical skills, your physical surroundings and equipment, and specific ways to process calls. In later chapters, you will learn techniques for maintaining a positive attitude and record-keeping skills, all of which are important for the TSR.

Effective Use of Telephone Equipment

Here are some practical, easy-to-use techniques for the telephone. How you use the telephone has a bearing on the impression you make. Also, your physical surroundings are important; they influence your thoughts and your moods as well as your efficiency.

Avoid Distracting Noise

Since the telephone is an efficient receiver of sound, you must be sure no annoying sounds are transmitted to people when you are talking to them. Your company will be responsible for providing you with a workstation or office that does not have distracting background noise. Ordinary office background noises are acceptable if they are not overly loud.

It is your responsibility to be certain that you are not the source of any distracting and irritating sounds. Habits, such as clicking pens, tapping pencils, shuffling papers, and chewing gum, can make irritating noise for the person on the other end of the line. Remember to avoid them.

Chewing gum can impair the sound of your voice. Certainly you would not eat food or drink coffee or soda while trying to talk on the phone. The sound of your chewing, which the phone will pick up, would not be appealing to the prospect/customer. If your company does allow smoking, avoid audibly exhaling smoke. Better yet, try to smoke between calls rather than during calls. Since your mouth is so close to the other person's ear, the sound of your exhaling will be loud and annoying. Think of it as the telephone equivalent of blowing smoke in someone's face.

Holding a Telephone

Hold and use the telephone in a way that will ensure that your message is clearly conveyed.

- Speak directly into the mouthpiece with your lips close to but not touching the instrument (two or three inches away).

- Avoid holding the receiver braced between your shoulder and your ear. This distorts your voice and makes it difficult for people to hear and understand you. Many companies provide TSRs with headsets so they will be able to speak clearly, avoid tense neck muscles, and their hands will be free to write or enter data on a computer.

Avoid Clutter

There are two kinds of clutter that weaken the performance of a TSR: physical clutter and mental clutter. They are related, influencing and being influenced by each other.

Physical Clutter

If your workstation is cluttered, you will not be as efficient as you could be. That inefficient clutter will be reflected in many negative ways: slow response time to prospects/customers, loss of important information, and misdialing, to name just a few. An uncluttered work area is as important as the smile on your face.

With an uncluttered desk, you will be able to find what you need when you need it. For example, when you reach for the phone, either to make a call or to answer a ring, you also reach for a pen and paper (message pad, order blanks, service order, record sheets, catalogs). Even when the workstation is automated TSRs often have to jot down information on a scratch pad to enter after the call is completed.

With practice, this will be as automatic as the smile with which you greet each call. Keeping written records of the calls you make is an important part of a your job as a TSR. (See Chapter 7.)

Keeping the caller waiting while you search for an order form, a pen, or anything through a clutter of other objects will not give a good impression.

Keeping your area organized requires you to pay attention to details. The payoff is that you will be able to give all callers the attention they deserve and expect. And you will always be ready to write down telephone numbers, orders, and other important information, and just as important, find it later.

Mind Clutter

A main cause of inefficient, unfocused performance by a TSR is mind clutter. **Mind clutter** is what you get when your mind, often unconsciously, fills up with distracting material that is irrelevant to the calls you are making. A main reason for this mental clutter is your **peripheral vision**. Peripheral vision refers to your eyes' ability to perceive visual images not only from in front of you but also from both sides.

Peripheral vision is helpful in driving, when you use it to keep an eye on traffic to either side of you as you watch the road ahead. But peripheral vision is not so helpful when it feeds distracting images into your subconscious mind without your knowledge. In a cluttered office, peripheral vision generates mind clutter.

Your peripheral vision picks up the clutter around you and feeds it into your subconscious brain. This clutter is like static in a radio. Just as the static in a radio prevents you from receiving the signal clearly, static in your mind keeps you from thinking clearly.

Imagine that three or four projects and some paperwork that need to be done are piled on one corner of your desk, several slips with phone messages waiting for their call-back are on a spike in another corner, an engagement book is open just off center with important meetings clearly marked, and miscellaneous items not necessary for your work are strewn about.

Although you are not aware of it, your eyes are taking all this clutter in as you talk on the phone. Add to this the fact that you think at a rate of 400 to 600 words per minute but talk only at a rate of 150 to 170 words per minute. That leaves a lot of time for your mind to drift while you are on the phone. Stimulated by what your peripheral vision is picking up, it is thinking such things as:

- *Oh my gosh, when am I ever going to get that project done?*

- *I hate paperwork!*

- *There aren't enough hours in the day to call all those people back.*

- *I'm not prepared for that meeting.*

These subconscious, negative thoughts clutter your thinking, making you less effective and slower with responses to prospect/customer objections and questions. Sales suffer as a result. A feeling of hopelessness comes over you and fatigue sets in. You feel, "What's the use, it won't get done." You miss the sale or make an error on a service call. Your production is down.

Mind Clutter Control

Although peripheral vision cannot be shut off, you can be in charge of what it allows into your mind in two ways: by minimizing the clutter in your area and by surrounding yourself with things that are inspiring and pleasing to look at.

Organize your work area so that you have a clear working space, with tools—pen and paper—readily available. Those items that you use can be kept in sight and stacked neatly to one side so they do not clutter your working area.

Use Written Material—You are in charge of mind clutter when you keep written material pertaining to your work. Consolidate bits of written information so they do not get lost. When you have a task to do, do not jot it on a loose piece of paper. Keep a folder or notebook for tasks to be done.

A desk calendar with room to write tasks is useful when you need to remember to do a task on a specific date. Written "to-do" lists are very helpful. Besides keeping track of your responsibilities and avoiding clutter, you experience a sense of accomplishment every time you finish a task and cross it off the list.

How not to use a phone: Surrounded by distractions, holding it wrong, not concentrating.

Have Positive Images in Sight—If you keep positive images in sight (pictures of family or friends, posters of a vacation spot you enjoyed, awards), your productivity will be increased rather than decreased. These images stimulate positive thoughts.

Procedure for All Calls

To establish a service-oriented approach quickly, develop and follow a procedure on all calls, whether incoming or outgoing. **Procedure** refers to a set sequence of steps to follow. For TSRs, call procedure should be second nature.

Identify Yourself Immediately

The most important step in the procedure is to identify your company and yourself immediately upon making or answering a call. Since the greatest difference between visiting with someone over the phone and face-to-face is that you do not see each other over the phone wires, the need to identify yourself seems obvious. Strangely, some people seem unaware of this and do not introduce themselves.

Not introducing yourself in face-to-face meetings is so discourteous that you would rarely be guilty of it. Since the other person cannot see you when talking on the telephone, an immediate introduction is not only courteous, but necessary. Putting people through a guessing game is not courteous. Even if you think the person will recognize your voice, it is better as a matter of courtesy and practicality to identify yourself.

You can use the opportunity of introducing yourself to convey your sense of pride in yourself and your company and its products or services by speaking in clear, confident tones. You do this even if the person who answers your outbound call is not the person you were calling. Do not be coy with a secretary. Introduce yourself clearly and confidently to sound like someone the decision-maker would want to talk with.

Introducing yourself immediately projects a businesslike image and has a positive psychological impact on the other person. When people hear you give your name, their usual response is to identify themselves, even if they had planned not to.

This saves time because you do not need to ask for a name. It also helps you avoid tension. When you must ask for a name, people sometimes make you feel uncomfortable, implying it is not any of your business. You can often avoid this by giving your name immediately and triggering the spontaneous response in which the other person identifies him or herself.

Use Your First Name

You can give either your full name or just your first name when making or receiving a call. Which you do depends on company policy, the image you want to project, and how you feel most comfortable. It is a good idea to use your first name whenever possible.

- *Good morning, Ellis Real Estate. This is Betty.*

Giving your *full* name assures people they are speaking to a real person. Using your *first* name helps them remember it and encourages them to use it. There are other good reasons for using your first name:

- It is generally easy for prospects/customers to remember and to use a first name.

- It creates an atmosphere of friendliness and informality that makes prospects/customers feel comfortable.

Using your name makes telephone contact as personal as face-to-face contact because people are immediately aware that they are talking to a real person, not an impersonal voice. When you say your name in a friendly manner you tell people that you enjoy your profession. With outgoing calls, it is a simple courtesy to identify yourself immediately. With incoming calls, you are showing callers that you are glad they called and are ready to help them in any way you can.

Know and Use People's Names

Use the other person's name. This is one of the most important techniques in telemarketing. When you hear the name, immediately write it down so you will not forget it. If it is unfamiliar, spell it phonetically as you write it, so you do not mispronounce it. If you are unsure of the name or its pronunciation, do not hesitate to ask the person to repeat it. People like saying their own name and they like hearing it—pronounced correctly.

Even if both you and the prospect/customer are speaking clearly, you can benefit from the use of the time-tested Bell Telephone Alphabet, shown here. You can insure against error—and botched sales—with such phrases as, "Was that A, as in Alice?" or "That's P, as in Peter." This is especially helpful in spelling unfamiliar names, streets, towns, and so on.

A—Alice	J—John	S—Sam
B—Bertha	K—Kate	T—Thomas
C—Charles	L—Louise	U—Utah
D—David	M—Mary	V—Victor
E—Edward	N—Nellie	W—William
F—Frank	O—Oliver	X—X-ray
G—George	P—Peter	Y—Young
H—Henry	Q—Quaker	Z—Zebra
I—Ida	R—Robert	

When possible determine the pronunciation before you speak with the decision-maker. Following are situations you can expect to experience and some suggested ways to determine the correct pronunciation.

When the decision-maker is not the person who answers the phone:

If party answering says only "Hello," select one of the suggested openers and without pausing ask for the pronunciation.

General Openers
- *Hello, I'm* (name) *with* (company) *and I'm calling for* (first and last name) [NO PAUSE] or
- *Hello, I'm* (name) *with* (company) *and I'm calling for* (Mr./Ms last name) [NO PAUSE]

Suggested wording for asking the correct pronunciation:
- *Am I pronouncing the name correctly?*
- *Is that how* (his/her) *name is pronounced please?*
- *Would you please give me the correct pronunciation of* (his/her) *name?*
- *Before speaking with* (him/her), *I would appreciate your help in pronouncing his/her name correctly.*

Asking for the pronunciation without pausing makes the difference. If the person who answers the phone has said his or her name and it is still unclear, courteously ask them to repeat it one more time so you will be certain of saying it correctly.

When the decision-maker answers the phone:

You know it is the decision-maker answering, but the individual speaks quickly and does not give a name.
- *Hello,* (name), *this is* (name), *with* (company). *Am I pronouncing your name correctly?*
- *Would you please repeat your name so I'm clear on its pronunciation?*

If the decision-maker uses his/her first name when answering the phone, remember not to take the liberty of using the first name until you have asked and received permission. *Always* say "thank you" after the person gives you the correct pronunciation. *Always* immediately write it phonetically on your records so you will not forget. *Always* refer to your records before calling the person.

Hearing their name has a calming effect on people. It reduces nervousness and increases their willingness to listen. Your correct pronunciation of names conveys the message that you care about people, see them as individuals, and are ready to meet their needs.

First Name/Last Name?

Most people, when asked, "Do you prefer I call you by your first or last name?" will choose to have you call them by their first name. This is good because using the first name retains attention for eight seconds. Using the last name retains attention for four seconds, provided it is the original last name or a name the person has been using for a long time—through marriage, for example, such as the married senior citizen who has been addressed by her last name for many years. A familiar last name may even retain the attention for as much as six seconds.

Use Names Naturally

Use the person's name often, but do not overdo it. Using it in every sentence would be overdoing it. Use it naturally as in a conversation with a friend. Use it just before you give important information, ask a question, or move into the closing. It is natural to use a name when you are about to voice an important thought and you want your listener's full attention.

Once you begin to know your regular customers, you will be able to recognize their voices. You can acquire many phone business friends by recognizing people over the phone and addressing them by name. These friendly feelings will result in even more business, which benefits everyone.

Returning Calls

If you need to look something up and return the call later, ask for the best time to call back. This will save time and the person called will be receptive, because you will be calling at a convenient time for them.

Ending Calls

End calls in a courteous, businesslike way. Avoid both ending calls abruptly and talking longer than necessary. Telephone courtesy dictates that the one who places the call end the conversation. If you have placed the call, be careful not to take up too much of the other person's time. Make sure you have finished all your business and that the other person is also finished, then promptly and graciously say good-bye.

If the other person has placed the call, let her or him end it. You can, however, offer trial ending statements that will allow you graciously to move the conversation to a close, such as,

- *Thank you for calling, Mr. Jones, I'll take care of that immediately.*

Another good way to do this is to confirm that you have all the necessary information. Use this opportunity to make sure you have spelled the caller's name correctly, have the right phone number (and address if you need it), and that you both know what the next step you take is going to be.

The way to be sure that the telephone call is closed *courteously* is to make certain that the other person hangs up first. Then you will know that you have not crashed the receiver in someone's ear, or missed some important last remark.

Procedure for Inbound Calls

You will be receiving as well as making calls. Answering the phone can become so routine that many people begin to do it poorly out of boredom. You have no doubt called a company and heard the person answering rattle off the company name so quickly, or in such a mumble, you were not sure you had reached the right company. Guard against answering the phone in this manner.

At the first ring of the bell, even before you pick up the receiver, begin using positive telephone techniques. The first step in a service-oriented approach is to take a deep breath to relax and smile when the phone rings, so that you are ready to greet the caller in a friendly, courteous manner.

Always give your company's name and your name clearly at a moderate rate with an alert, smile-in-your-voice tone as if the caller were the first one today and you are happy to take the call.

Answer Phones Promptly

To make a good first impression, whenever possible answer the phone by the second ring. Keep your telephone within easy reach rather than hidden behind papers or other objects (clutter again).

Promptly answered phones project efficiency. Slow pickups or unattended phones create a poor image. Slow pickups irritate callers. Waiting time always seems longer than it actually is. Five rings of a telephone take only 30 seconds, but to a waiting caller they can seem like 30 minutes.

This is especially true if you handle complaint calls on a regular basis, since callers are already feeling frustrated and impatient.

If a caller has already been transferred, she or he is already impatient, so answering promptly on an extension is particularly important. If there will be a delay before anyone can pick up on the extension, and you are the original receiver of the call, give frequent progress reports to the caller on hold.

If a call is to be transferred, you will generally have company guidelines to follow. When you take a transferred call, answer with your name just as if you were answering initially. If you know the caller has been kept waiting while you finished another call, say "Thank you for waiting" after identifying yourself.

Here are some effective, positive remarks you can use when taking incoming calls. The simple courtesy of giving your name promptly and clearly is an important factor in projecting a service-oriented approach.

Answering a company phone
Thank you for calling (company name), this is (first name).

(Company name), (first name), how may we help you?

(Company name), this is (full name) speaking.

Answering your own phone
(your first name, or your full name with emphasis on the first).

Answering a department phone
(Department name; your name): *Accounting, Joan Williams.*

Answering another person's phone
(Other person's name, your name): *Joan Williams's office, Deb Smith speaking.*

Answering a transferred call
(Your name). First, give a salutation, such as "Good morning." Then, you can give your first name or your full name (no titles), emphasizing your first name.

Hold the Hold

Sometimes the pressure of work makes it necessary to juggle several actions. This is particularly true for TSRs whose job requires them to take calls coming in on advertised 800 numbers.

One result of this has been the growing use of the hold button on the telephone. When it is unavoidable, always give the caller the choice to hold or not by saying something like, "Do you have time to hold for a minute? Thank you." A poor way to answer the phone is to give the company's name and yours, and without pausing add something like, "I've got to put you on hold, please wait." and immediately hit the hold button. Unless people really need something from your company, you can bet they will hang up. And if they do hang on, they are not going to be in a happy frame of mind.

Try to give them a chance to indicate whether they want to hold. That polite, soft sell pays off. People will wait more patiently if they feel they have been given a chance to decline. Otherwise, they will be doing a slow burn.

When you must put someone on hold, check back with them at least every 30 seconds saying, "It will still be a little while. do you wish to continue to hold?"

Respond to Customer's Opening Statement

Customers often open a conversation with a question. Try to answer with a positive statement rather than another question. If the call is for information or to place an order, be ready to take care of that need or transfer the call to the right department.

If the call is a complaint or a problem, be calm and understanding. Correct the situation if you can. Dissatisfied customers can be retained if they discover someone is concerned about their needs. A follow-up call later to be sure that they are happy with the outcome reinforces this impression of concern and helpfulness. The word-of-mouth advertising of satisfied customers is invaluable.

How to Screen Calls

At times the person being called is not available. Tactful *screening* will avoid offending the caller. Examples would be:

- *"I'm sorry, Mr. Williams isn't available right now. Is there any way I can help you (be of help)?"*

Service-Oriented Skills 89

- *"May I transfer you to another (person/department)?"*

When someone is not available, using the contraction *isn't* softens the sound and helps eliminate the perception that he or she does not want to receive the call.

When you take messages, confirm the spelling of the caller's name, the phone number, and any other message.

Write everything down. Never assume that the person being called has the number. Write it down. This avoids having to look it up or, even worse, not being able to return the call because the number has been forgotten.

Make sure that the message is complete and intelligible. Although it may seem trivial or obvious, it is important to the other person, so be careful and complete when writing it down.

Procedure for Outbound Calls

When receiving incoming calls, you want to be prepared to handle requests without knowing in advance exactly what the call will be about. For outgoing calls, you can prepare and plan.

By planning the conversation, you create a businesslike impression and avoid the need for additional calls. Planning saves time and money.

Have Number Ready

Be certain that you have the right number before placing a

Telephone courtesy requires respecting the privacy of your colleagues by not being too explicit when answering phone calls.

Too Explicit

She is in conference with Mr. Johnson.

Helpful

She is away from her desk at the moment. I expect her back soon. May I have her return your call?

Too Explicit

He is on a long distance call to Chicago.

Helpful

He is talking on the other line. May I please have your name and number so he can return your call?

Too Explicit

He left early to play tennis.

Helpful

He is out of the office for the afternoon. He will be back in the morning.

call. Keep a list of frequently called numbers available. Do not rely on your memory even if you think you know the number well. The digits are easily transposed in your mind. It takes about eight seconds to locate a number on your frequently called numbers list, 22 seconds to get a number from a telephone directory, and 55 seconds to get a number from directory assistance.

Have Name Written Down

Equally important is having the name of the person you are calling written down. You may think, "How could I not know who I'm calling?" The fact is, though, it is possible for your mind to wander while the phone is ringing, causing you to forget whom you have called.

This danger is especially strong for those who spend a great deal of time talking on the phone to many different people. Write the person's name down and have it in front of you so you do not have the embarrassment of groping for it when he or she answers.

Place Your Own Calls

Place your own calls as much as possible. Having someone else place calls implies that your time is more valuable than that of the person you are calling, which may seem rude or arrogant.

Remember Time Differences

If you are calling to other states, remember the difference in time when placing calls. You will find a time zone map in the front of your telephone directory.

There are four time zones in the continental United States (Hawaii and Alaska are in still different time zones). There is a one hour difference between each zone, with the time getting earlier as you move west, later as you move east. If it is 9 a.m. in New York City, it is only 8 a.m. in Dallas, Texas, 7 a.m. in Denver, Colorado, and 6 a.m. in Los Angeles, California.

Save Time

Always identify yourself and the business you represent immediately to save time and to make it unnecessary for the other person to ask who is calling. Project efficiency and planning by courteously giving the reason for your call at once.

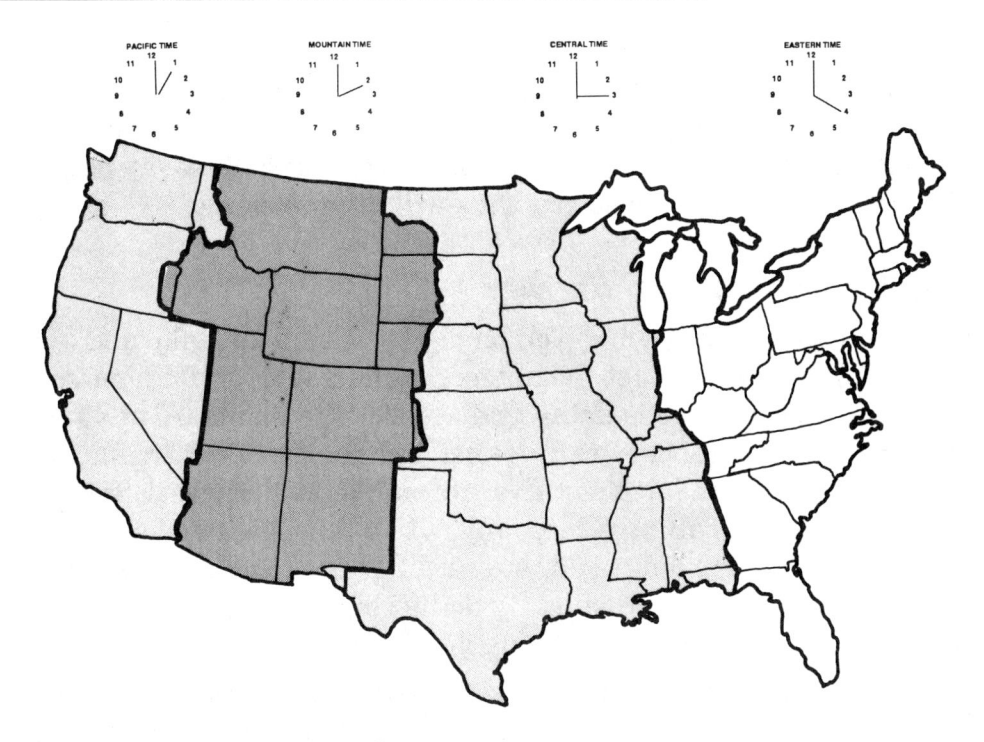

Time zones in the continental United States.

Ask for Time

As soon as you have identified yourself and your reason for calling, ask if the person has a few minutes to spend with you. You have no way of knowing what people are in the middle of when you call, so it is only courteous to ask if they have time to talk.

Many TSRs, fearful of receiving a "no," just start talking. This loses sales because the other person may be irritated at the rudeness of the interruption or feeling stress about other matters and, in short, not receptive.

Courteously asking for the person's time is a Win-Win situation. You obviously win if the answer is "Yes, I have the time," because then you can make your presentation. If the answer is no, you also win because you are quickly freed to make more calls. More important, you have allowed the person to say so without forcing her or him to interrupt or to wait impatiently until you have finished your remarks. You have not alienated the person and, most often, the person will give you permission to call back.

If the answer is no, suggest courteously some alternative times to call back:

- *Since that's the case, I won't take any more of your time now. May I please give you a call later today or would sometime tomorrow be better.*

Giving the other people a choice of times helps them make a decision. If you simple ask what would be a convenient time, you force them to make an effort to decide and they may just say forget it. When given a time to select, they will often pick one.

Give Person Time to Answer

Sometimes, especially when you have a lot of calls to make and are rushing, you might not let the phone ring long enough for a person to stop what he or she is doing and answer the phone. Always let the phone ring at least seven times before hanging up when placing a call to a home, and at least five times when calling an office. If you know you are calling a company with a busy switchboard, you might let the phone ring six or seven times because the operators could be busy with other calls. By doing this you are less likely to hang up just as the phone is being answered.

Letting phones ring too long wastes your time and could have negative results. In most situations, people at home can get to the phone in seven rings, and if they cannot, it is usually because they are doing something, such as taking a shower, that makes reaching the phone difficult. A person pulled reluctantly to the phone by its persistent ringing will hardly be in a receptive mood.

Master Benefits of Answering Machines

More and more homes and small offices are using answering machines. These are convenient for people who must be away yet do not want to miss their calls. Many people, however, resent the answering machines so much that they do not give any message when invited to do so and simply hang up. They may feel this is getting back at the person in a small way for having such a machine, but it is pointless behavior.

TSRs using the soft sell approach look upon answering machines as totally positive. People frequently use answering machines to screen unwanted calls, and since such people would be unlikely prospects, the machines serve you by helping to identify qualified prospects.

Rapport/Credibility Builder

When a prospect without an answering machine is not in, he or she is not aware of your effort. The answering machine invites you to leave your name, number, and message, and promises to call back as soon as possible. In leaving your message begin by saying that you appreciate the opportunity to leave a message. The prospect will be pleased because most people either leave no message at all or express annoyance at the machine.

Time Saver

In several kinds of telemarketing, a rule of thumb is that you should make three attempts in a day or week to reach a prospect who does not answer. The answering machine reduces the number of attempts that need be made.

Vocabulary

Mind Clutter
Peripheral Vision
Procedure

Discussion Questions

1. How do the two kinds of clutter cause you to be inefficient and ineffective?

2. What is the most important step in the telephone procedure? Why is it important? What positive effects does it have?

3. Why is it important to use the other person's name? Discuss how and when to do this. Explain how you can avoid mispronouncing or misspelling names.

4. Describe steps you can take to ensure that incoming calls are answered with a positive, service-oriented approach.

5. What are points to remember when screening calls? Give an example of how to screen and how not to screen calls.

6. What are some things to remember when you are taking messages?

7. How do you prepare for making an outgoing call? Describe other steps you can take to ensure that your call projects a positive, service-oriented attitude.

8. What are the benefits of answering machines? How should you deal with them when they answer your calls?

9. Discuss experiences you may have had with TSRs who were not service-oriented. Has a "service-oriented approach" ever affected your buying decision?

Activities

These activities will help you use telephone equipment effectively and develop a service-oriented approach.

A. Using Equipment Effectively

A well-organized workstation eliminates physical and mental clutter. Draw a diagram of a workstation, including tools you use regularly: pen and paper, to-do lists, names and numbers of people to call, phone book or list of numbers, calendar, material on your product/service. Also include motivational pictures, mottoes, and so on, that you might have in your workstation.

B. Developing Procedures for All Calls

Practice the procedures you read about for handling all calls.

Identify yourself immediately. Discuss why this is important and give examples, from your own experience if possible, of being misled when you weren't sure who was calling.

Use your first name or your full name. Discuss situations when it would be preferable to use your full name instead of just your first name. How do you feel when you get a call from an unknown person who uses your first name?

Know and use the other person's name. Practice saying your classmates' full names until you can pronounce each one naturally and correctly.

Return calls. Discuss how you have felt when someone failed to return a call, or did so much later, or without the information you had requested.

C. Handling Incoming Calls

How long is a minute? Work with a classmate or in a group with one person being the timer. The others should close their eyes and raise their hands when they think a minute has gone by. Note how people's perception of time differs—and how few judge correctly.

Answer phones promptly. How do you feel when you place a business call and no one answers? The next few calls you make, time how long it takes before the phone is answered. Do you know, for instance, that the person you are calling has a big house, works outside or in a busy office, and needs more time to answer the phone?

Attitude and Persistence

Two Control Factors

Two Steps to Change Your Thinking Mood

Three Kinds of Affirmations

Complaints

Vocabulary

Discussion Questions

Activities

Chapter 6

Developing a Positive Attitude

Upon completion of this chapter, you will be able to

- recognize how positive and negative thoughts affect one's attitude,
- identify two control factors that influence the mind programming process,
- use a simple two-step process to change negative into positive thinking,
- identify three kinds of affirmations,
- develop ways to reduce complaints.

In this chapter you will read about the importance of attitude in your success as a TSR—or in anything else, for that matter. You will also learn how negative thoughts can influence your attitude without your conscious awareness. But, you can control those negative thoughts and, in effect, program your brain, much as one

Overcoming negative attitudes is one of the biggest challenges TSRs face.

programs a computer, to maintain positive thoughts that will lead to positive action.

TSRs, of all salespeople, are the most susceptible to negative thoughts. This is because of the large number of contacts they make in a day. A face-to-face salesperson can see as few as 3 to 4 people in a day. TSRs meet many times that number.

With so many contacts, it is only normal to encounter some people in a negative mood. We sometimes tend to take another's bad mood or rude manners as a personal affront, and become irritated.

Since you always want to be pleasant over the phone, it is important that you keep any feelings of irritation or annoyance to yourself. Often we stuff these feelings into the back of our minds. This, however, can cause negative thoughts, which influences your behavior. You unconsciously project these feelings on the next phone contact, which is not good for business.

What has happened is that you have unconsciously programmed your mind—in this case, in a negative way. You can program your mind consciously, however. Until you become aware of this programming process, it is only an involuntary action and not a resource to use in your telemarketing career.

Attitude and Persistence

How your brain is programmed affects your attitude, and 85 percent of your success in anything you do depends on your attitude. Only 15 percent of your success is based on your education and your skills. Even if you have a doctorate or 40 years' experience in some area, your attitude is still the overriding influence on your success. Being in control of how your brain is programmed is therefore crucial.

> **P**olite persistence is the key to telemarketing success. This fact is underscored by these statistics printed in the *Sales and Marketing Management* magazine.
>
> 48 percent of salespeople quit contacting a prospect after the first contact if they do not say YES.
>
> 20 percent more quit after the second contact.
>
> 7 percent more quit after the third contact.
>
> 5 percent more quit after the fourth contact.
>
> 4 percent more quit after the fifth contact.
>
> And yet:
>
> ✓ 75 to 80 percent of all new business is written AFTER the fifth contact!

In selling, a positive attitude is essential. Every salesperson, in face-to-face selling or in telemarketing, encounters rejection. Those who become negative and give up early do not succeed. Those who maintain a positive attitude and persist succeed.

Learn Polite Persistence

It is important for you to make periodic contacts with prospects to try, politely and persistently, to sell your product/service. Persistence will pay handsome dividends for both you and your company. It can be learned, but it requires a positive attitude.

Persistence, more than anything else, increases sales. A TSR who courteously asks for permission to call back at a later date after a prospect says "no," and then does call back periodically (every three months, for instance), will establish a strong prospect base, and will increase his or her total number of sales.

The following sections describe how a typical prospect thinks of the first call, how the prospect thinks of the calls that follow, and why polite positive persistence is important.

Initial Call

During the initial call, the prospect may think, "Another salesperson; I'm just not interested in listening." So the prospect says something like "not interested" in reply to the request for an order.

An effective TSR realizes that this reaction is to be expected, does not develop a negative attitude, and courteously asks permission to call again.

At least 80 percent of the time, the prospect will say, "Okay." For the prospect thinks, "Well, I got rid of that salesperson. She won't ever call back." And indeed, nearly 50 percent of salespeople do not call back.

Second Contact

An effective TSR with a positive attitude records the date on which to make the next contact and makes it, using a lead-in that gently reminds the prospect of the previous conversation. For instance, "I'm calling because when we talked back in May, you mentioned that I could touch base with you in July."

The prospect thinks, "Yes, I did tell this salesperson that she could touch base and, by golly, she did. I don't know about the product she's selling, but she is certainly dependable."

The prospect may still not grant an appointment or buy the product/service, but he or she has begun to have confidence and trust in the salesperson. In almost all cases, the prospect will agree that the TSR can touch bases again in a couple of months.

However, about 20 percent of salespeople think, "There have got to be better prospects out there," and will not call again.

Third Contact

The effective TSR calls again in another two or three months. The prospect is likely to remember the TSR and will probably talk a bit this time about the product/service. Some will even agree to a sale or to an appointment. Others will at least be interested enough to ask for literature or agree to have literature sent to them.

It is important to consider that many people are careful decision-makers. They dislike being rushed, and they distrust people they feel are pushy. They need to read literature about a product/service, weigh all the pros and cons. Once they make up their minds, they are likely to be pleased with the product/service and to be loyal customers. However, many salespeople who have gone this far now develop a negative attitude and give up.

Fourth Contact

The fourth contact can be made three days to a week after literature is sent. Now the TSR asks if the prospect has any questions about the literature and proceeds into a sales conversation. The prospect might:

- Agree to a free trial offer, if the TSR mentions one.
- Agree to try a small amount of a product, or try something with a money-back guarantee.
- Grant an appointment.
- Say, "I want to think about it." (In fact, more than half will probably say this.)

At this point, more salespeople give up—although they are close to success. Many prospects who say they "will think about it" mean what they say; they will indeed think about the product/service. Salespeople with a negative attitude regard "will think about it" as a put-off, and cross the prospect off their list. They do not realize that many people *have* to think things over as a vital part of their decision-making.

Fifth Contact

When a TSR makes a fifth contact a few days later (saying, "...to see what your thoughts are"), many will buy the product/service. Others will want more time to think. These people may be careful decision-makers, and of course many salespeople give up on them.

These people may well have money to spend, partly because of their careful spending habits. They may really want the product/service. They need, however, considerable time and encouragement to buy it. Once they do buy, they are very likely to be satisfied, loyal customers. The TSR who keeps a positive attitude and uses polite persistence will succeed.

Two Control Factors

To take control and develop the positive attitude essential to success as a TSR, you should be aware of two factors that influence your mind programming process:

1. Your subconscious mind does not know the difference between reality and fiction.

2. Your conscious mind can only think one thought at a time and you can control what that thought is.

The Self-Fulfilling Prophecy

Your subconscious mind believes everything you think, say, or hear. For example, if, just prior to making a phone call, you say or think, "This is a waste of time, I know this person isn't going to buy anyway." your subconscious mind will believe you.

Your subconscious mind influences your attitude and, consequently, colors your actions. When it hears a defeatist thought, it slows down your thinking process. You become less enthusiastic, you do not think of answers to objections as easily, your voice loses its tone of confidence. The result will most likely be the "no sale" you anticipated. This is known as the **self-fulfilling prophecy**, which means that what you expect to happen does, *because you expect it to*.

Fortunately, the self-fulfilling prophecy also works with positive thoughts. If you have positive thoughts, the chances of achieving positive results increase. Therefore, learn to program your mind with positive thoughts about expected results before making calls.

Take Control

Think about *control*: "Your conscious mind can think only one thought at a time and *you can control* what that thought is." You introduce positive or negative thoughts into your brain all day long. You can control this process by screening negative thoughts, such as "I'm not going to make the sale," "I'm so tired," "I hate paperwork," and replacing them with positive ones.

Here are some of the benefits you will enjoy when you develop the habit of positive thinking:

More Energy

More Accomplishment

More Confidence

Need of Less Sleep

More Fun

Less Fatigue

More Happiness

More Creativity

No Procrastination

More Enthusiasm

Good Health

Clear Thinking

More Effectiveness in Sales

Better Time Management

Maintaining positive thoughts is a challenge because so many things are expressed in negative ways. For example:

- We call it a stop light, though it is green as long as it is red.

- We say the glass is half empty when it is half full.

- News headlines are mostly negative: Murderer loose—Tornado kills 30—Senator under investigation. Positive news is treated as not news at all: "No news is good news."

- Weather forecasts predict "partly cloudy" days instead of "partly sunny" days.

This bombardment of negative material can influence your own outlook; be on guard against it. When you say or think negative things, you program your subconscious mind negatively, whereas when you say or think positive things, you program your subconscious mind positively. So stop yourself when you begin to think negatively. Turn the negative words into positive ones:

- I just know I'm going to make this sale.

- I'm wide awake and alert.

- I can handle paperwork.

Since your subconscious mind does not know the difference between reality and fiction, it will believe these positive statements to be true, and it will stimulate positive physical and mental reactions in you that will yield positive results.

Affirmation: Self-Influence

Affirmation in this text refers to the act of suggesting something definite and specific to yourself in a regular, systematic, constructive, and positive way so as to program your subconscious mind positively. This is also known as **autosuggestion**.

Effective affirmations follow these four simple rules:

1. Affirmations are expressed in the first person ("I").

2. Affirmations are expressed in the present tense. (The subconscious mind exists only in the "ever-present now.")

3. Affirmations are expressed as positive statements. (Your subconscious mind needs something concrete to respond to. It cannot imagine the negative condition, "I am not afraid of the phone when making a sales call," because this signifies the absence of a feeling. "I enjoy using the phone to communicate with prospects/customers" is a positive statement that your subconscious mind can visualize.)

4. Use affirmations regularly over a month or more. Using the affirmation technique for two or three days and then stopping will not bring about the desired results.

Two Steps to Change Your Thinking Mood

Your subconscious mind accepts as true whatever the conscious mind hands it. If the thought is positive, the subconscious mind is creative. It creates ideas, hunches, and intuitive insights that help you be productive and happy.

If the thought is negative, the subconscious mind generates fuzzy, unclear thinking, and can even cause ill health. Negative thoughts are destructive, just as positive thoughts are dynamic and creative.

Use these two steps to turn negative thoughts into positive ones:

1. Learn to notice when you think or talk in a negative way so you can change immediately.

2. Generate a positive thought and concentrate on it for one to three minutes.

Many times negative thoughts are so strong that it is hard to think of anything positive. Therefore, it is important to prepare ideas in advance that you can concentrate on when this occurs. The activities at the end of this chapter will help you come up with some positive ideas to use when you need them.

After one to three minutes of positive thinking, you are ready to return to doing something productive. Remember—"Beginning is half done." It is important to get started on something productive to keep your negative thinking to a minimum.

> When the conscious mind grasps a thought of any kind (negative or positive), it causes a corresponding vibration in our voluntary system of nerves in the conscious mind. Because of this, a similar current is generated in our involuntary system of nerves in our subconscious mind. This is our body's way of physically handing our thought over to our subconscious mind for it to use its powers to create or destroy. The whole process takes only about three minutes.
>
> (Dr. Joseph Murray, *The Power of the Subconscious Mind*)

Three Kinds of Affirmations

Affirmations can be grouped into three different categories: *verbal* affirmations, *visual* affirmations, and *activity* affirmations.

Verbal Affirmations

Spoken or thought expressions of positive encouragement—affirmations in words—are known as **verbal affirmations**. These include self-made affirmations and borrowed affirmations.

Self-Made Affirmations

Positive statements you think up for yourself are **self-made affirmations**. For example:

- I love the phone.
- I enjoy visiting with people.
- I feel calm and confident on the phone.

Borrowed Affirmations

Affirmations based on material you have discovered in other sources are **borrowed affirmations**. Place such positive messages or ideas where you can see them in your telemarketing station. For example:

- The me I see is the me I'll be. (Maxwell Maltz)
- Success doesn't come the way you think it does—success comes because of the way you think. (Dr. Robert Schuller)
- I feel healthy, I feel happy, I feel terrific. (W. Clement Stone)

Visual Affirmations

Visual aids to help program your mind are **visual affirmations**. Place positive, motivational pictures, clippings, drawings, or awards and ribbons where you can see them in your telemarketing station. These can be of things you have accomplished, special people you admire and want to be like, things you want to do or have, places where you have been or would like to visit.

Your mind will absorb this material and produce energy, creating the desire to accomplish what you want and increasing your enthusiasm level. As you read, the subconscious mind is the seat of the imagination, and it uses visual imagery in its thought processes. By surrounding yourself with visual affirmations, you give the subconscious mind specific, concrete material to work with in creating a positive sense of accomplishment and satisfaction.

Activity Affirmations

Affirmations you have recorded to listen to are **activity affirmations**. They can be self-made or borrowed. (See "Affirmations to Use" for specific suggestions.)

Just as the subconscious mind works better with visual images, it is also more affected by spoken than by written words. Spoken words go deeper and more quickly into your mind, directly affecting your subconscious. Each time the words are repeated, they are planted more firmly in your brain.

Affirmations to Use

Here are several affirmations grouped into two categories. Record any that you like. Fill the tape by repeating them. Listen for five minutes three to five times a day, for no less than six weeks, as part of your campaign to program your mind for a successful career in telemarketing.

I Love Telemarketing; I'm a Terrific Salesperson

1. I'm proud to be in telemarketing. The profession is growing by leaps and bounds. There is unlimited potential for me, and I love being in on the ground floor of something so big.
2. I am a terrific salesperson. I start with a positive opening, then ask if I am calling at a good time. People are warm and friendly. I know they appreciate my asking before I go on.
3. Because I'm a doer, a person of action who gets things done, I will be successful.

4. Once I know it's fine to go on, I ask questions about the person's wants and needs. I use only the soft sell approach. I'm good at this type of communication.

5. I'm excited and enthusiastic about my company and what it offers. I know all the benefits of its products and share them with my prospects/customers with pride. My customers trust me and have confidence in me because I'm honest.

6. I realize that people like to have help in making decisions, so I always ask for the order. This gives people a chance to clarify their thinking by asking questions or giving objections. It's exciting when people do either, because then I know they're interested. I know these are buying signals, so after each answer I ask a trial closing question.

Think of the phone as a friend and partner.

7. I'm excited and enthusiastic about my work and the business phone friends I make. My attitude is positive.

I Love the Telephone

1. I know the phone is an extension of two human beings: myself and the person on the other end of the line visiting with each other. I am relaxed and comfortable on the phone—just as comfortable as face-to-face with a person.

2. I am eager to start making phone calls each morning; I know that the people on the other end of the line are equally eager to hear how my product, service, or idea will improve their world. Because I know this, I feel confident every time I dial.

3. I look forward to meeting more and more people by phone and making many business phone friends. I enjoy dialing the number because there is a warm and friendly person on the other end of the wire.

4. I know that there is a certain mystery—curiosity—about a phone call that stimulates people's interest. I am the one in control. They have given me the time, and I am prepared with an initial benefit statement to gain their interest immediately. Being prepared gives me confidence.

5. *The phone is my best business buddy*—Every time I hear the phone ring—whether it's an incoming call or an outgoing call—it's

ringing up sales. The phone increases my sales. I know that the more people I tell about my product/service, the more I sell.

6. *The phone is my best business buddy*—because it helps relieve stress from financial pressures. I love making more sales, which benefits my prospects and earns me money. I enjoy having the money I need to pay my bills, and I enjoy having money left over to do fun things. I love having extra money in the savings bank.

Complaints

One type of call that gives you opportunities to practice your positive attitude skills is the complaint call. There are several aspects to handling a complaint: attitude, note taking, and voice control. (You will read more about note taking in Chapter 7, and about voice control in Chapter 10.) Handling complaints will never be a joy, but it can be made more pleasant.

Remember that the subconscious mind produces fuzzy, unclear thinking when negative thoughts are present. This is why people may be unreasonable when registering a complaint.

You are at an advantage. Your thinking is clear—unless you allow fear to take over, in which case there will be two people with fuzzy, unclear thinking. This is disastrous. One reason for immediately returning a call to someone with a complaint is so that your fear and the other person's anger do not have time to build up.

When handling a complaint, avoid placing blame. Resist the temptation to pass the buck. Bad-mouthing the company, a supplier, or some other person only weakens your own credibility.

Keep in mind that however angry the caller sounds, the anger is not directed at you. What the person wants is for you to understand the problem, take charge of the situation, and correct the problem. Listen for the *content* of the message rather than the tone. Use affirmations to emphasize your calmness and composure.

Once you decide what you are going to do, make sure it is done quickly and smoothly. Then follow up with a phone call to make sure things have been taken care of to the customer's satisfaction.

Responding to Complaint Calls

A professional TSR will always be ready with positive responses to complaints—a **cushioning technique**—that project a helpful reaction. If you are not ready, you might react to the anger in the caller's voice and use words that make the situation worse.

See the list on page 112 for suggested phrases to reply to a customer with a complaint. Select ones that fit your style to practice with. As you gain experience you will memorize appropriate phrases tailored to your needs and approach.

Some of the more powerful responses begin with phrases such as "I agree . . . " and "I understand . . . ." These immediately show your concern and willingness to help. "I understand . . ." is probably the best because it is safer. That is, when saying "I agree . . . " you may be committing yourself or your company to a line of action that would not be suitable nor required. Always be sure you get all the facts before making a commitment. You can, however, say something like:

- *I agree with your feeling you should call. Now let me make sure I have all the facts so we can correct the situation.*

Or,

- *I agree, you want to spend your money wisely, and. . .*

Using the words "I agree," and then repeating exactly what the caller has just said, is a good cushioning technique.

One of the smallest words in the language can play a big role in your cushioning technique: YES. Beginning your response with "yes" quickly sets the positive, helpful image you want and lets the caller know you are interested in helping, not arguing.

Be careful with some innocent-sounding transitional phrases that may elicit a negative psychological reaction. For example, if after saying, "I understand . . . " you introduce your points with the transitional phrase "on the other hand" or, "however" you send up red flags that you are about to disagree. A better transitional phrase would be, "May I explain our position...."

Reducing the Number of Complaints

The most important way to handle complaints is to *prevent* them. This means making sure ahead of time that things are being taken care of to the customer's satisfaction. In this way you will reduce the number of complaints you eventually have to deal with and also help the customer keep a positive attitude.

The best way to reduce the number of complaints is to communicate clearly and make only promises you can keep. For example:

Whenever you are handling a complaint call, here is a list of what you want to remember to do:

1. Slow down your rate of speech. (See Chapter 10)

2. Lower the volume of your voice. (See Chapter 10)

3. Express regret for any misunderstanding. Find a point of agreement. Use a cushioning phrase. (See list beginning on page 112.)

4. Tell the caller that you'll be writing down the details to help you resolve the situation.

This sample response to a customer registering a complaint combines steps 3 and 4:

I'm really sorry about this, (name). We definitely want to resolve the situation in the best way possible. Why don't you tell me about it and I'll jot it down to make sure I have all the details.

If the caller speaks too quickly:

Could you speak more slowly, please? I'm a slow writer.

5. Ask intelligent questions and listen attentively. TAKE VERY ACCURATE NOTES. (See Chapter 7.)

6. Read back to the person what you've written, using a lead-in statement such as:

To be sure I clearly understand what happened, let's review what you've told me. Please stop me if you have something to add or change.

This step has a calming effect on the caller because it provides an opportunity to clarify while demonstrating that you are listening and want to solve the problem as quickly as possible.

7. Tell the person making the complaint what corrective action you are planning. Make a commitment that can be kept.

8. Fulfill the commitment and follow up to make certain things have been taken care of to the customer's satisfaction.

1. Identify the prospect/customer's expectations *before* making any promises. For instance:

P/C: *When will it ship?*

TSR: *I'll be happy to check that for you, (name). How soon do you need it?*

2. If there is *any* possibility that expectations cannot be met, check to see what can be done. Add a margin for safety based on your experience. Quote a range of expectations, not a specific fact. For example:

TSR: *Although I'm unable to give you an exact date of arrival because it's coming from our supplier's stock in (city), I can say that it will be sometime between (date) and (date) based on past experience. Does that sound okay with you?*

Note: In any situation, first tell the person what you cannot do, *then* say what you CAN do! This may sound like the opposite of positive thinking, but it is not. It prevents false expectations, so the positive message of what *will* be done is received clearly.

3. Sell the right product by asking questions to determine wants and needs of the prospect/client.

4. To ensure that everything is clear, read back the order to confirm quantity, description, price, terms, address, delivery date, and any other conditions.

5. Service sells, so promptly return all calls. Some will be complaints, but handling them quickly and effectively retains customers.

6. Put all orders in writing to avoid any misunderstanding. Use such items as:

- A signed contract
- A purchase order
- Letter of intent
- Order acknowledgement

Below are cushioning phrases you can use to let customers know you will be handling their complaints as quickly as you can. Practice them, selecting the ones you feel most comfortable with. Have them ready, either in your head or on a sheet of paper, to use when complaints arise to help you keep a positive attitude and help the customer have one as well.

1. A good point, (name), and I'll be happy to clear it up.
2. Good thinking, (name). I didn't explain that too well. Let me try again.
3. Good for you—you're on top of things.
4. I thought exactly the same thing.
5. I understand how you feel. Many of our *customers* have felt that way before they *found* out that...
6. I understand why you feel that way.
7. I know how you feel, (name), and you're right.
8. I'm glad you brought that up.
9. In many cases that's true.
10. It's easy to understand how you might think so.
11. I see the position you're in, (name). Might... make a difference?
12. I see your point.
13. I see what you mean.
14. I can relate to that.
15. I certainly understand how you feel.
16. I can sympathize with how you feel.
17. I see your position.
18. Let's see what you think after I explain.
19. Normally, that would be correct. In this case the circumstances make it different.
20. Naturally, I can understand your hesitancy, which is why...
21. That's a good question.
22. There is much in what you say, (name).
23. That's a good suggestion.
24. That's understandable.
25. Under ordinary circumstances, you'd be absolutely right.
26. Well, I know what you mean. I felt that way myself.
27. What you say is really worth considering.
28. Yes, you're absolutely right. I agree with you.
29. Your idea certainly shows good thinking.
30. You may be interested to know I once thought the same way.
31. Yes, many people feel as you do.
32. Yes, I can relate to that.

By following these steps, you reduce the number of complaints you ultimately have to deal with, thereby relieving yourself and the customer of stress. Think of these as external ways to maintain a positive attitude, complementing the internal method of affirmation and self-influence.

Vocabulary

Activity Affirmations
Affirmation
Autosuggestion
Borrowed Affirmations
Cushioning Technique
Self-fulfilling Prophecy
Self-made Affirmations
Verbal Affirmations
Visual Affirmations

Discussion Questions

1. Explain why positive, polite persistence is important to you as a TSR.

2. What is a self-fulfilling prophecy? Why do expectations about phone calls become self-fulfilling prophecies? What role does the subconscious mind play in the success of sales calls?

3. How can the subconscious mind and the self-fulfilling prophecy be used for positive effect in telemarketing?

4. What is the first step to change your thinking from negative to positive? How long do you have to make the switch, and why?

5. What is the second step to change your thinking from negative to positive? What is a major obstacle to overcome in that process? How can it be dealt with?

6. What are the four characteristics of an effective affirmation? Why must affirmations be stated in positive terms?

7. What are the two kinds of verbal affirmation? What are some ways they can be implemented? Discuss various self-made affirmations of your own that you think will contribute to your positive attitude and successful calls.

8. How do visual affirmations help develop a positive attitude? What kind of visual affirmations might you keep in your work station?

9. What are activity affirmations? Why are they more effective than simply reading a written verbal affirmation? Why is repetition so important?

10. Share any experiences you may have had or know about where a positive attitude led to success.

11. How does dealing with complaints involve a positive attitude? How does having a positive attitude help? How can dealing with complaints help you keep a positive attitude?

Activities

Do these activities individually.

A. Change Negative to Positive Thinking

Chances are you have had a negative thought about someone or something in the past day or two. Did you try to use the two steps described in the text to generate positive thoughts? If you did not, do so now. Keep the technique in mind for the future.

B. Use Three Kinds of Affirmations

First, think of three positive statements that you have thought up yourself or borrowed from someone else. Repeat them to yourself during the course of several days.

Next, find two visual affirmations. If they are small, you might consider carrying them in your wallet. If they are larger, put them near where you work or study. After several days ask yourself if these affirmations have helped you develop a positive attitude. If they have not, replace them with new ones.

If you have a tape recorder, prepare a taped affirmation as well. Again, after several days, you might want to change it if you feel there are others that would be more effective.

C. Reduce Complaints

Write, in detail, a description of a complaint you have received and how you handled it, or of a situation you complained about and how it was handled.

What techniques did you use to calm the person down? (Or how were you calmed down?) Note any techniques that you think will be helpful in handling future complaints.

With a partner, role play a complaint call using responses similar to those found on page 110. Use phrases from page 112 to demonstrate your concern to the complainant.

Essential for Service

Record Management System

Call Tracking Equipment

Note-Taking Techniques

Complaints

Call Preparation

Vocabulary

Discussion Questions

Activities

Chapter 7

Keeping Records

Upon completion of this chapter, you will be able to

- recognize the need for written records,
- develop an effective telemarketing record management system,
- identify equipment and forms for telemarketing record systems,
- use note-taking skills for keeping records,
- improve complaint handling procedures with accurate record-keeping skills,
- use records to prepare for future calls.

In this chapter you will learn about record keeping. All professional telemarketing operations maintain daily records of their activities. Telemarketing managers use these records to determine where and when revisions need to be made in scripts, sales presentations, or any other part of the system.

Records are important for keeping track of what has happened with each account over a period of time. You may be in contact with the same customer for months or even years. By keeping records you are able to assess changes in attitude and buying habits that can help improve your sales. For all these reasons, maintaining call records is an important part of your job as a TSR.

Essential for Service

There are other reasons for maintaining records. TSRs handling mostly inbound calls will find record-keeping skills essential in providing the service that will keep old customers and attract new ones. Whether the calls are for service, information, or to place orders, a set of records will enable you to refer to previous calls, handle new developments, and track prospect/customer's buying history. Handling complaints is another reason for keeping records. Complaint calls can be stressful, and you are liable to forget what has been said if you do not keep notes. Furthermore, you will need to remember how you promised to help, and the nature of the complaint to pass along to the service department.

Record Management System

Obviously, given the number of calls made in a day, you cannot possibly remember the call information and call activity of every contact. (**Call information** refers to the time, length of call, name of person called—general information about the call. **Call activity** refers to the specific content: purposes, results.) Therefore, a **record management system**, computerized or manual, to compile a record of all calls, is essential.

In large or small operations, telemarketing managers maintain the record management system and they need the individual TSRs' records to compile the overall reports. Consequently, all TSRs must keep accurate records of the calls they make.

Depending on the size of the department, the record management system may be a 4 x 6 card file or state-of-the-art computer technology. There are many telemarketing **software** packages (computer programs) from which companies may choose, if they decide to automate. Companies with automated record management systems usually give TSRs on-the-job training in using them. Not all companies doing telemarketing use automated systems, but the trend is moving rapidly in that direction. For this reason, computer skills are valuable for a TSR.

Although individual computer software packages vary, a large part of learning them is learning basic computer skills. If you use an automated system, understanding the principles behind any record-keeping system is still important. Computer programs tend to be based on the same principles as the manual system they were designed to replace.

Call Tracking Equipment

The principles of call tracking and record keeping are the same for all types of calls. The exact nature of the information to be preserved varies, however, depending on whether the primary function of the TSR is to make outbound calls or to take inbound calls.

In outbound calls, records need to include information about the total number of calls made, how many of them were successful *contacts* (as opposed to busy signals, wrong numbers, no answers), and the call activity of those calls that were successful contacts.

Inbound call records include the number of calls taken; the reason (the type of inquiry, the particular product/service being asked about); whether the TSR is to call back or send information; orders taken with the quantity and amount. Elements may be added or subtracted, depending on the telemarketing application.

Once a prospect has made a purchase, a file will be started that can then be accessed each time the person calls for information or service, to make a complaint, or for any other reason. It is also available to the TSR making any necessary outbound calls, such as a customer retention call a few days after the purchase has been made. This file becomes an important part of the records to be used in any type of telemarketing call.

Outbound Calls

There are three basic elements you will need in order to keep accurate, convenient records of outbound calls:

1. Reminder Calendar

2. Call History Sheet/Card

3. Call Tracking Form

Reminder Calendar

The **reminder calendar** is a desk calendar in book form (6 x 8 inches or larger), showing the year, with one day per page, on which you write, under the appropriate date, the names of prospects/customers you are to call. The reminder calendar contains only information that you must remember at a particular time. All other information is stored on the call history sheet, which is described in the next section.

Desk calendars can be purchased or made by writing the dates at the top of sheets of three-hole paper (front and back) and putting the sheets in a notebook. (When writing dates always include the day of the week: Wednesday, 10/20/9-.) Divide pages in half vertically with a line to create a space for pertinent notes.

Some desk calendars come with the hours printed down the left side of each page. This can be useful for keeping track of the times when you have promised or want to call people. It is a good tool for scheduling your day. If you make your own desk calendar, put times down in 15-minute segments beginning, for example, at 9 a.m. and ending with your last working hour, such as 4:30 p.m. Leave the first and final 15 minutes open for updating records. See the sample in Figure 7-1 on page 121.

When you make arrangements to call a prospect/customer, record the person's name, company, and the time on the relevant page in your reminder calendar. As you put together your list of calls to make each day, refer to the calendar for the accounts you need to call back. Another piece of information on this reminder calendar is the time to send a note to people prior to the next call. You record the name with an *N* for *note* five days before the date of the call back to ensure they will receive the note prior to the call.

Other information can be recorded in the reminder calendar. For example, if a prospect/customer says he or she will call back on a certain day, or during a specific time period ("sometime next month"), you can mark this information down. Then, if the person does not call back, you can place a reminder call, leaving a comfortable space so it does not look like you are pressuring them.

Call History Sheet

The **call history sheet** consists of index cards or sheets of paper on which you record the call history for each account. The **call history** is the record of all the call information and contact activity for each account, from the time of the first call.

Wednesday 10/20/9-		
09:00		
09:15		
09:30		
09:45		
10:00		
10:15		
10:30		
10:45		
11:00		
11:15		
11:30		
11:45		
12:00		
01:00		

Figure 7-1. **Reminder Calendar**

Each sheet contains the name of the account (with pronunciation if necessary), phone number, company (where applicable), and address. Below this information you record the date of each call and the call activity that occurred. This can be simple—"NA," for "no answer"—or detailed for easy recall of what happened, what needs to be done. If you need a lot of space, just add another sheet.

When a prospect/customer promises to call you back, record this information, including the time, in your reminder calendar, as well as on the call history sheet. (See the sample in Figure 7-2 on page 123.) Rather than trying to write the same information twice while you are talking, make a habit of marking the call history as you talk and then write the name on the reminder calendar after the call. It only takes a few seconds and streamlines accessing account information later. The name you write on the reminder calendar will be how your call history sheet/card is filed.

The reminder calendar and the call history sheet together give you a comprehensive, easily accessed record of the history of every contact. When you prepare to call a prospect/customer, everything you need is filed alphabetically, so you do not have to root through piles of scrap paper and hastily-scrawled notes to find important information.

In Chapter 5 you read of the importance of avoiding clutter, and of having the name, pronunciation, and phone number of the contact in front of you before making the call. The call history sheet gives you this and other things as well. It enables you to refer to previous conversations, so you are always in touch with the prospect/customer's needs and wishes, what has already happened, and so on. This projects efficiency and consideration, which your prospect/customer will appreciate.

You might also use the call history sheet to record observations about the person you are calling—likes and dislikes, for example, or your visual image of the person—to help you establish a friendlier rapport. Written reminders refresh your memory before the next call. If you use the call history sheet this way, reserve a section for it and design the sheet accordingly. Write legibly. Often one TSR will make another's calls during peak periods. Refrain from cluttering the margins with doodles that make it hard to read.

Filing Call History Sheets—Store call history sheets alphabetically in a box or file drawer. Use separate headings for different kinds of prospects/customers. For example, you will always want to have a backlog of new prospects. File these in their own section after you have sent the note of introduction and before the first contact. Make a tab for referrals not yet called. The rule of thumb is that no call history be filed alphabetically until the first call has been made and a follow-up date recorded on the reminder calendar.

Each morning spend a few minutes going through your reminder calendar and other records, pulling the call histories and prospect sheets/cards of the people listed on your reminder calendar and put them behind your "Call Today" section at the front of your file drawer or box. Store blank forms for future call history sheets in the back of your file so you can reach them easily.

Reminder Tags—Attach adhesive-backed notes to sheets, cards, or folders that need special treatment. Attach them so that they stick up above the line of folders in the drawer or box, with the message facing you when you open it. Since pads of this adhesive-backed notepaper come in various colors, you can use them to color-code tasks and priorities as needed.

Using these reminder tags lets you keep the call history sheet neatly in its place no matter what follow-up action is required. Accounts requiring special treatment are immediately apparent because of the reminder tags. For example, you can use colored tags to flag files to be called back at a specific time the same day.

Contact: Name:	
Title: Pronunciation:	
Phone: Extension:	
Company:	
Street Address:	
City: State: Zip:	
Comments: (Anniversaries, birthdays, family)	

Date	Call History

Figure 7-2. **A Sample Call History Sheet or Card.**

Write the time on the tag and refile the sheet in the "Call Today" part of your file for easy access. Use a different color to indicate that someone is going to return your call. Write the person's name in large letters at the top of the tag, and refile the sheet alphabetically. When the call comes in you can find it quickly. Another color might be used to indicate that some action needs to be taken. On the tag write, for example, "send brochure," "write letter," "write proposal." Leave the tag on the call history in the file as a reminder until you complete the necessary action. Many TSRs write the date the action is to be completed.

Call Tracking Forms

Call tracking forms are used to record the number of calls made and decision-makers reached (as opposed to busy signals, no answers, call back requests), what products or services were sold, what appointments were made, and any information needed for the particular telemarketing application. They are a log of essential phone activity over a given period of time. Tracking forms serve two basic purposes. They allow you to monitor your performance,

124	Skills and Attitude

File call history sheets according to the type of call. Keep today's calls in the front of the drawer.

and they provide management with a means of analyzing the results of the applications.

Call tracking forms are designed with a particular call purpose in mind. Calls for appointments, for example, would be tracked with a form that records the number of solid and tentative appointments. Sales calls would record the product or service that was sold, quantity, dollar amount, referrals, and information to be sent. At the bottom of each column totals are kept for the day, week, or whatever period of time the tracking form covers. Every form has columns to indicate busy signals, no answers, wrong numbers, disconnected numbers, call backs, and prospects who said they will call back. (See Figure 7-3, page 127.)

Leave a space in your totals row for number of attempts—how many numbers you have actually dialed, whether busy, wrong number, or whatever, during the time period. You might find it easier to make a separate column for this information, and, every time you dial a number, to put a check in it. Then, for the total, it is a simple matter to count the checks, rather than moving from column to column as you total each of the various other categories.

Inbound Calls

Prospects and customers usually make inbound calls for one of four reasons: to ask for information, to make an order, to ask for help with a product/service they have already purchased, or to make a complaint. In this section you will read about record keeping for inbound calls for information, order entry, and customer service. (The fourth category will be dealt with separately in the "Complaints" section of this chapter.)

The call tracking equipment you will use for inbound calls is essentially the same as that for outbound calls; however, the structure of each element and the emphasis placed on it will differ.

Record keeping for inbound calls is as important as for outbound calls. Until the prospect calls in, the company has no record of the person's name, address, or phone number, and no idea of what potential market the caller might be in. Keeping good customer service activity records helps in retaining their business.

Some companies make a point of getting this basic information right away, as soon as the call is answered, while others may wait until the prospect has shown some interest in a particular product. In any case, it is vital to the success of the telemarketing operation that accurate records be kept.

This becomes even more apparent when you consider that many telemarketing operations that use the inbound direct method are doing some form of mail-order selling—taking orders over the phone and sending the product/service directly to the customer.

This means that everything from sales figures to inventory control depends directly on the records the TSR and telemarketing management keep. Some companies—those that make certain

---

Use standard, easily understood abbreviations to write down important information quickly. Listed below are some of the common ones that TRSs use.

Attempts: Numbers dialed (used on a call tracking sheet to total the calls made during a day or some other time period)

NA: No answer

WCB: The other person will call back

B: Phone was busy

TA: Tentative appointment set

FA: Future appointment. The prospect/client gave the TSR permission to call back in a specific amount of time

DM: decision-maker

CB: Call back; person called not available

SA: Solid appointment set

Info: Wants information

CTC: Call to confirm (When a tentative appointment is made, a call to confirm is made to see if the timing is still okay.)

products to order, following customer specifications—even require accurate telemarketing records for production to function smoothly. The records TSRs keep are used by production to schedule their activities and to adjust for customer requests.

Reminder Calendar

TSRs handling inbound calls use the reminder calendar much less than those making outbound calls. With inbound calls, the reminder calendar serves mainly to remind you of prospects/customers who have asked to have information sent, and of the few outbound calls that need to be made (mainly follow-up and customer retention). Inbound calls do not require scheduling the way outbound calls do.

Planning, of course, remains essential. In this case, however, the plan is for the presentation that will be made once the prospect/customer calls in.

Call History

As you read in Chapter 3, a large number of inbound calls are generated by traditional marketing methods such as direct mail and media advertising. Prospects/customers call in for information or to place an order. When a call comes in, a call history for that prospect/customer is started, or added to if one already exists.

The call history will include, as with outbound calls, the name (with correct pronunciation), address, and phone number of the account. Each time the prospect/customer calls in, a note is made in the call history of the date, the reason for the call, and action taken, if any. For example, one entry might note that a call came in for information about a possible upgrade of equipment, and that the prospect/customer asked to be called the following week. The call back would go on the reminder calendar.

Call Tracking Form

Information recorded on the tracking form summarizes the day's calls. The information it contains is of great importance, not only to the telemarketing operation itself, but also, depending on the nature of the business, to the inventory, production, and service and fulfillment departments as well.

Call tracking forms for inbound calls include information on the number of calls, the purpose of each call, the call activity, and future actions to take, if any. The purpose might be as simple as

BEFORE DM IS REACHED							AFTER DM IS REACHED				
A	B	NA	WN	DIS	CB	WCB	P/S	QTY	AMT	REF	INFO

Figure 7-3. **Sample Call Tracking Form** Headings can be modified to suit various call applications. Totals are recorded in the bottom row. (A=Attempt; B=Busy; NA=No Answer; WN=Wrong Number; Dis=Disconnected Number; CB=Call Back; WCB=Contact will call back; P/S=Product/Service sold; Qty= Quantity; Amt=Dollar Amount; Ref=Referral; Info=Information to send.)

"Information" or "Order Entry," or it might be broken out into numerous subcategories: the type of inquiry (for example, graded according to probability of sale); the product or service being asked about, whether the TSR is to call back later or send information.

Information on orders will vary with the type of product/service, but will always include the quantity, and dollar amount of the sale. (See the sample in Figure 7-3 on this page.)

Note-taking Techniques

When taking notes AND KEEPING RECORDS, it is unnecessary to write down every word the prospect/customer says. That is not the point of taking notes, and doing it will hinder, not help, your listening. What you want to do is to get the main points, the key ideas, and the vital information.

Use the "telegraphic" style for taking notes. That is, eliminate what are called "function words"—prepositions, articles, auxiliary verbs (be, do, have)—and other secondary words wherever possible. Think of how newspaper editors write headlines, and use the same technique for recording the caller's information: "Washing machine broken—leaks on floor!"

Taking notes does not mean that you should write down what the caller says word-for-word; rather, it means that when you use the telegraphic style, the important verbs and nouns you choose will be the ones the caller has used.

Record vital statistics, model numbers, and, of course, names, addresses, and phone numbers in full.

Eliminate Silent Letters

Besides eliminating unnecessary words, you can speed up your note taking in the way you write words using some common sense rules. They do not always produce results that make sense immediately. In the list below, for example, you may not recognize the words on the right, but each was produced by following the simple rule, "eliminate silent letters."

- snow = sno
- tie = ti
- leave = lev

With a little practice you can become as accustomed to this style of writing as to normal English spelling—which, after all, is quite unpredictable itself! Your notes will be quicker and take up less space, leaving you time to concentrate more fully on what your prospect/customer is saying.

Because it is possible that another TSR may be making the follow-up calls or that your telemarketing department exchanges calls, make certain you rewrite the necesssary information so others can read it.

The sections below give suggestions for other common sense rules you can use to speed up your note taking and improve your listening skills.

Write What You Hear

You read about spelling unfamiliar names phonetically in Chapter 5. You can extend this practice to familiar words, since phonetic spellings are usually shorter than standard ones: "phone" spelled phonetically would be "fon," which saves you two letters. This may not seem like a lot, but when you are working to get down everything the prospect/customer is telling you, the saved letters will add up quickly.

Use Abbreviations

Words of two or more syllables can be easily abbreviated in a number of different ways. A common one is to eliminate all the vowels, leaving only the consonants: the word *consonants* becomes *cnsnts*, *vowels* becomes *vwls*. Another method might be to record

> Besides abbreviations, there are common typographical and other symbols you can use to speed your note taking. Examples include:
>
> @ for *at*
>
> $ for *money*,
>
> % for *percent*,
>
> + or & for *and*,
>
> ↑ ↓ for *up* and *down*,
>
> ? for *question* ("Mr. J. had ? abt new svc."),
>
> # for *number*.
>
> There are also mathematical symbols that come in handy for abbreviating sentences. Some of the most useful ones are:
>
> ≥ for *greater or equal*
>
> ≤ for *less than or equal*
>
> ⇒ for *so, therefore*
>
> ∅ for *none* or *nothing*,
>
> ∈ for *There is...*,
>
> ∉ for *There is not....*

only the first or the important syllable, especially with frequently used words: *frequently* becomes *freq.*, *psychology* becomes *psych.*, "attend" becomes *att.*

The danger with abbreviations is that you might forget what they stand for. The second system is especially dangerous, as in the case of an abbreviation like *rel*. It might stand for *related to, relationship, religion, relegate, relapse, release, relevant*—any number of words. Be careful to use only abbreviations whose meaning will be obvious later, from the abbreviation itself or from the context (*rel.* followed by the word *to* narrows the possible interpretations considerably).

Many industries, businesses, schools, and other institutions with telemarketing operations will have their own special abbreviations. Depending on the type of telemarketing application you are doing, you will no doubt be using some of these in your daily calls. (See the box on page 125 for some common telemarketing abbreviations.)

When you use abbreviations, do not try to follow the other rules, such as eliminating silent letters. Doing this plus shortening the word could easily make it unrecognizable.

Complaints

The need to handle complaints in a timely, courteous, and effective manner is another reason to master record-keeping skills. By keeping notes during a complaint call, you can keep the conversation from becoming too stressful and also make sure you deal with everything the customer has called about.

Usually callers with complaints are upset and distracted. The tension can fluster even the most experienced telemarketer. If you tell a caller you will be writing down their complaint so that you can resolve the situation, you immediately establish your concern. You also slow the conversation by saying you need time to write everything down. The heated rush of the complaint subsides, and the caller begins to think more clearly. This is to everyone's advantage.

Write as quickly and legibly as possible. Try to get as much as you can, writing it *in the way it is said*. When people are upset and not thinking clearly they do not fully realize what they are saying. If you take the information down in your words, they will not recognize it as having come from them. However, they will relate to the words they themselves use.

Then say, "To make sure I have everything right, I'll read it back. Please correct me if I'm in error." This helps calm the person. It shows you were really listening and were interested enough to remember the exact complaint. This persuades the caller that you will take an active interest in solving the problem. When people hear their words read back in a calm voice, they often realize they may have exaggerated somewhat. This gives them an opportunity to clarify without feeling foolish. (Do not, of course, repeat thoughtless or rude comments that may have slipped out. Read only information related directly to the product/service.)

Once you have determined what the problem is, review with the caller the corrective action you plan to take. *Keep a written record of what you have promised.* This is important because people will tolerate and forgive one mistake, but two will leave a wound that is next to impossible to heal. The customer is usually lost. Keeping a record also enables you to follow through quickly and thoroughly. If the complaint requires referral to a service department, take detailed notes about the exact nature of the problem, so as to be able to give the service personnel as much information as possible. This will facilitate handling the complaint and contribute to keeping the customer satisfied.

Finally, make a note on your reminder calendar to check on the prospect/customer in a few days, to make sure everything has been taken care of. The personal touch of this follow-up contact helps cement the relationship.

Call Preparation

Keeping records allows you to prepare for subsequent calls. Polite persistence, as you have read, is at the heart of successful telemarketing. You must be prepared to speak with the prospect/customer a number of times before making a sale. Each time you talk, you will want to build on what has already been established. You will want to continue developing your rapport, giving information that you have found since you last spoke, answering questions raised during the last conversation.

If you have taken good notes—writing down questions the prospect/customer asks, checking off elements of the presentation you have already covered, jotting down relevant details—you will have a solid foundation on which to base your next call. You can use this information as part of your opener: "I found the answer to that question you had about the service contract, Bill." Thus, call preparation can be seen as the final step in record keeping, or record keeping as the first step in call preparation. You are moving through a cycle of steps.

Vocabulary

Call Activity
Call History Sheet
Call History
Call Information
Call Tracking Form
Record Management System
Reminder Calendar
Software

Discussion Questions

1. What are some of the reasons it is important to keep accurate records?

2. What is *call information*? What is *call activity*? Explain why is it important for TSRs to record this information.

3. How is the information recorded for outbound calls the same as that for inbound? How are they different?

4. What information should be recorded on the reminder calendar? What should not?

5. What is a call history sheet and how is it used?

6. Why is record keeping so important for inbound calls?

7. What does the call tracking form do? What sort of information does it record for inbound calls?

8. Why is record keeping important in handling complaints?

9. How is record keeping related to call preparation?

Activities

The following exercises will help you appreciate the need for written records.

A. Recognize the Need for Written Records

Describe at least four reasons why written records are important in telemarketing. For each reason think of one or more difficulties that would arise if no records were kept.

B. Using Forms and Abbreviations

Using the sample call tracking form as a model, draw up a form appropriate for the kind of telemarketing you do or would like to do. You can use the company you created in earlier activities. Work with a partner, one acting as TSR, the other as prospect/customer. Role play various situations—not interested, please call back, send information, take an order—and practice using abbreviations and note-taking techniques.

Unit III
TELEPHONE FLUENCY

Chapter 8—Using Words Effectively

Chapter 9—Creating Your Own Style

Not All Words Are Created Equal

Context

Connotation

Categories

Pronunciation

Articulation

Vocabulary

Discussion Questions

Activities

Chapter 8

Using Words Effectively

Upon completion of this chapter, you will be able to

- employ telephone fluency skills to prevent misunderstandings,
- use *context*, *connotation*, and descriptive words for a favorable reaction in the listener,
- identify six categories of telemarketing words, and their impact on listeners,
- recognize the importance of correct pronunciation and clear articulation,
- avoid common errors of pronunciation and articulation.

In all aspects of telemarketing, whether telesales or teleservice, words are the major tools with which you work. Your choice of words and how you say them will profoundly influence your effectiveness. The words you use to create images in the listener's mind—images of yourself, the company, and the product—take on a tremendous importance. In this chapter you will learn to choose words, and ways to ensure correct pronunciation and articulaton.

Using correct **pronunciation** means using the standard, accepted sounds, while having good **articulation** means producing sounds clearly, distinctly and smoothly. Another word for articulation is **enunciation**. For instance, the correct *pronunciation* of "seine" (a net used in fishing) is *sane*, not *sen* or *seen*. The word "fishing" is well *articulated* (or *enunciated*) when the final *g* is audible (not "fishin"), yet not uttered too harshly either.

You will want to have good articulation, and at the same time sound natural and relaxed, not tense or irritated with over-articulated speech. You want to articulate clearly so you will be understood, and so you do not sound sloppy, lazy, or inconsiderate. On the other hand, you do not want to sound unnatural.

You might enunciate a word clearly, but pronounce it incorrectly, or pronounce it correctly, but articulate it indistinctly or awkwardly. For example, you might say the word "often" perfectly clearly, articulating every sound, but mispronounce it by inserting the *t*, which should be silent. Or you might pronounce difficult words correctly, but so sloppily that you cannot be understood.

Ultimately you will combine the right words with good articulation and correct pronunciation for smooth, effective delivery.

Not All Words Are Created Equal

The true meaning of a word is in both your use of the word *and in the listener's understanding of the word*. Always be aware that what you mean by a particular word may not be what the listener understands by it; be sensitive to words' psychological impact. Even simple words such as "old" and "young," "easy" and "difficult," "large" and "small" can mean different things to different people:

- To an 80-year-old grandmother a 50-year-old man is "young," while to his children he may seem very old indeed.

- A computer manual's instructions may be "easy" to a technician, but impossible to a new user.

- A room in a house or an apartment may be "large" to one person and "small" to another, depending on the size of the rooms in their respective homes.

Be Specific

One effective way to avoid misunderstandings is to *be as specific as possible*. Avoid vague words like "large," "small," "fast," or "slow." Replace them with precise information whenever possible—the exact dimensions of a product; the minutes a task takes to complete.

> In telemarketing Mark Twain's famous adage is especially appropriate: "The difference between the right word and the almost right word is the difference between lightning and the lightning bug."

Of course you want to use descriptive terms as well, to help the prospect/customer visualize the product/service and understand how it will be useful. Be specific when the person has expressed interest and wants more detail. In the opening stages of the conversation use descriptive language with an emotional impact.

Try for Balance

Try to strike a balance between specific language and descriptive language. Use descriptive language to give life to the statistics; use the specific information to give impact and credibility to your descriptions. For example:

- *I think you will find that this computer fits your needs. It has a 40 megabyte hard disk. That means you can store a large amount on the disk—hundreds of pages—so you won't be moving floppy disks in and out all the time.*

- *This sleeping bag has been field-tested at minus 20 degrees Fahrenheit. You'd be able to sleep out in this on just about the coldest winter night in New England.*

Context

The meaning of a word is not just in the word itself, it is in how and when the word is used—the **context**. An obvious example would be a word like "expensive." If you are selling shoes, one hundred dollars might be "expensive." If you are selling cars, one hundred dollars is not even in the ball park. For another example, consider a word like "memory." A salesperson offering a special deal on buying film uses "memory" to imply preserving images of happy occasions. A computer salesperson, on the other hand, means something quite different by the same word, which in this case refers to the computer's power or storage capacity.

External Factors

Context can mean external factors that influence the use of the word, as in the examples already given. It can also refer to changes within the same situation. The opening steps of a telesales call, in which you use expressive, descriptive language, is one context; the later stage involving detailed information is another. Your choice of words depends on both kinds of context.

Other Aspects

There are still other aspects of the context that affect word choice. The rapport you have established with a prospect/customer—warm and friendly, businesslike and efficient—is an example. So is the type of call: complaint, telesales, appointment, etc. Choose your words to reflect the overall context of each call.

Let us say, for example, you are making calls for a landscape company offering a free estimate on all lawn installations. Your prospect/customer is interested, but she is a busy woman, and she wants you to get to the point quickly. You want to convey your company's speed, efficiency, and competence, without taking up too much of her time. You can give specifics—the method of seeding the lawn, the time and cost per square foot—using words that suggest efficiency, effectiveness, and ability.

On the other hand, suppose your prospect/customer is a homeowner whose main concern is the welfare and appearance of his lawn. He is retired and has plenty of time on his hands. The main thing you want to do in this case is reassure him that the work will be done conscientiously and carefully. In this case, you would use language that suggests care and thoroughness, rather than speed and efficiency—though he may be pleasantly surprised at how quickly the work gets done. You would let him know, with your choice of words, that the company shares his concerns.

Connotation

Besides their definitions, words have **connotations**—subtle differences in meaning that can significantly alter their effects. Consider the differences among the following synonyms for "fast:"

accelerated	swift
fleet	hasty
quick	rapid

If you sell computers and want to describe their speed, you would be well advised to avoid a word like "hasty," which *connotes* sloppiness and inefficiency. "Swift," on the other hand, suggests gracefulness and power. Similarly, "accelerated" suggests an added boost of power. These connotations appeal to listeners on a **subliminal**, or unconscious, level.

Categories

A helpful way to think about words as you develop telephone fluency is to organize them into categories that reflect their psychological impact on the listener. Six categories to consider are:

1. Descriptive vs. Nondescriptive

2. Technical vs. Nontechnical

3. Courtesy vs. No Courtesy
   (NOTE: This does not mean discourteous words, it means the psychological impact of using courtesy words as opposed to not using them.)

4. Positive vs. Negative

5. Soft Sell vs. Hard Sell

6. Conversational vs. Formal

The following sections look at the first four of these categories. Because of their importance, the final two—soft sell vs. hard sell and conversational vs. formal words—are treated separately in Chapter 9.

Descriptive vs. Nondescriptive

You read that specific words are often better to use than vague, general ones. This does not mean that your conversation should be all dry facts and figures. On the contrary, one of your goals is to stimulate the prospect/customer's imagination.

There is a big difference, however, between *descriptive* words and *vague, general* words. Concrete, specific language creates a more vivid image in the listener's mind than vague, abstract language. You can be detailed and clear without being dry or dull.

There are a few things to look out for when describing a product/service. On the one hand, you do not want to be too dry or dull. On the other, you want to avoid using worn-out, overblown, vague language that will not make any impression at all. The following samples illustrate different ways to express the same thoughts. (These are sentences that might be used in the persuasion step of a telemarketing conversation.)

SAMPLE #1: VAGUE/GENERAL

This computer is the best of its kind on the market. It does more than any other brand. It is easy to use, but the power it gives you is truly exciting. It is fast and efficient and will not cause problems.

SAMPLE #2: DRY, TOO SPECIFIC

This computer has 640K RAM with 340K expandable on the motherboard. It runs with a multi-task operating environment that permits the simultaneous use of several applications. Standard operating speed is 12 megahertz but it can be increased to 16.

NOTE: Part of the problem here is that the language is too technical. See the next section, "Technical vs. Nontechnical."

SAMPLE #3: THE GOLDEN MEAN

This computer has more working capacity than any other in the same price range (I'll be happy to give you the exact specifications if you like). If you buy from us, as a bonus you'll receive powerful software that allows you to run several kinds of programs at once—for instance, you could use a word processing program and an accounting program simultaneously.

Avoid Overused Words

Think of words like "beautiful" and "exciting." The ideas are good; however, because they are used so often, the words have lost their impact. We are conditioned to tune them out. Another example would be **superlatives**—words expressing extremes. Any word that ends in -*est* is a superlative (best, highest, fastest, newest), as are words like "perfect," "fantastic," "outstanding."

To convey what is appealing about the product/service, think of specific qualities. Is it efficient? Spacious? Convenient? What makes it that way? If it is beautiful, what makes it beautiful? Shape? Color? The way it fits together? Think about the product/service, analyze it, and share the results. Others cannot see what is in your mind. Your words create pictures in their minds.

Use Evocative Language

You can create vivid, enticing pictures in the listener's mind by using **evocative** words—words that evoke, or draw out in the listener's imagination, the appealing qualities of an object. (Think of the difference between "hasty" and "swift" described earlier in this chapter.) By using evocative, descriptive language to complement the factual information, you stimulate people's imaginations, and therefore their desire for your product, service, or idea.

The exciting thing about using evocative language is that it allows for flexibility and individuality. There is no *right* way or wrong way—there are just *different* ways. Everyone has slightly different associations with different words, which means that the particular descriptive language you use will always be a little different from what anyone else might choose.

Technical vs. Nontechnical

Every industry, whether insurance, real estate, or communications, has its own special terminology and abbreviations. When you are actively involved in your work on a daily basis, the terms, abbreviations, model numbers, and so on become second nature. Your complete understanding makes you a good salesperson.

A challenge is that you might tend to forget that not everyone knows as much as you do. Not everyone is familiar with all the terms and abbreviations. When you speak with prospects/customers, do not assume that they understand industry jargon, just because they do not ask questions. The truth is that many people do not understand but refuse to ask questions. They may be new in the industry and still learning. Or, they may have been in it a long time and not kept up. In any case, people do not want to show that they do not understand, because they do not want to appear ignorant. Instead of asking questions they say they are not interested, and the sale is LOST.

Another result of using a lot of technical words is that it conveys self-importance and a know-it-all attitude. You want to seem confident and knowledgeable, not pompous.

Try to avoid technical terms a prospect might not understand. If you do use them, explain them as you do. In avoiding technical terms or explaining them, be sure you do not sound as if you were talking down to the customer. If your tone of voice or choice of words conveys the impression that you think the person is not smart, you will almost certainly lose a customer.

> Descriptive words tend to refer to physical qualities—how things look, feel, sound, taste, or smell. Because they appeal to our senses, they have a more direct impact than words that merely express ideas: "warm" is often a more effective word than "pleasant," even if what is being described is not literal warmth. In the following list, all the words either refer to physical characteristics or to ways of doing something—action. How many can you use in your telephone dialogs/scripts? How many can you add to the list?
>
> | | |
> |---|---|
> | graceful | simple |
> | dynamic | swift |
> | elegant | lush |
> | cool | warm |
> | fragrant | sweet |
> | sturdy | light |
> | delicate | quiet |
> | smooth | soothing |
> | powerful | vibrant |
> | bright | solid |
>
> Note that each word describes a particular aspect of the thing it describes. How often can you replace words like "good," "nice," and "pretty" with more specific language? There are of course hundreds, if not thousands, of such descriptive words in the English language. Try listening to your own speech and others'. Make a note of the evocative words they use and places where they could have used one. As time goes on, your speech will become more descriptive and a more effective communication tool.

Courtesy vs. No Courtesy

This does not mean using courteous words *instead of* discourteous ones. You never use impolite words. The point is to use courteous words, such as "please" and "thank you," often and naturally.

People appreciate courtesy; it makes them feel special. And everyone deserves to be treated with respect. When you treat people with kindness and consideration, you not only make them feel good, but you also feel good about yourself.

Another aspect of courteous language is the way you let the person know you are paying attention. Listen—do not interrupt or assume you know what the other person is about to say. Respond in ways that take into account what the other person has already said. Do not flatly contradict the person or answer a different question from the one you were asked. Do not waste time repeating yourself once he or she has got the point. This is courtesy in any conversation, and especially telemarketing ones.

Here are specific ways for you to show courtesy, some of which will reflect what you have learned in other chapters.

1. Ask if the person has time to talk.

2. Ask permission to ask questions.

3. Use "please" and "thank you" wherever appropriate.

4. Use the person's name—first name unless there is an objection.

5. Ask permission to call back at an appropriate time if the person is not interested now.

Positive vs. Negative

When you speak you can be either negative, sowing gloom and doom, or positive, spreading happiness and hope. Conversations always seem to slant one way or the other—too often toward the negative. This makes maintaining a positive attitude a challenge, particularly because when we hear someone speaking negatively, our instinctive reaction is to speak negatively also.

Have you ever gone out feeling terrific only to meet someone who starts telling you about a negative situation, and how awful things really are? In a few minutes your terrific mood is gone.

Fortunately, the opposite can happen also. If you think and speak positively others will be inclined to do the same. You can influence people's thinking indirectly and quickly, so that they are unaware that you are doing it. Remember reading about how our subconscious mind can influence our attitude. You have about three minutes to change another's negative thinking to positive.

Take Charge

In any telephone conversation you want to move immediately to take charge to ensure that a positive mode is established. This is particularly important if the other person is being negative. This means taking charge in a polite, indirect way by being positive from the start and converting all negative comments the prospect/customer makes into positive statements.

To understand the technique, consider this scene. Sue calls a client whose son plays on the same school basketball team as hers.

Sue: *Hi, Don, Sue Carlson. That was some ball game last night! Didn't our team play well?* [positive]

Don: *Hi, Sue. I guess, but they made a lot of errors.* [negative]

Sue: *Yes, there were a few.* [agreeing but toning down the negative] *But the team effort on the whole was excellent, Don.* [positive]

Don: *Well, maybe so. But the coaches need to make those boys knuckle down.* [still negative]

Sue: [remaining positive and keeping control] *I'm sure with a few more practices they'll cut down the errors.* [NO PAUSE] *By the way, Don, the reason for my call is....*

Sue then starts programming Don's mind with positive information about her product/service. She keeps his attention by focusing on this subject and using positive, descriptive words.

Accentuate the Positive

A song that was popular several years ago made this point well: "You've got to accentuate the positive, eliminate the negative, and don't mess with Mister In-Between." There are so many thoughts that can be expressed negatively or positively:

- *We still have half the job to do.*

- *We are half finished.*

Even facts that are essentially negative or limiting can be stated in positive ways, if you think about it:

- *We only have three colors for you to choose from.*

- *You have three great choices of color.*

Always look for positive ways to say things. Concentrate on telling customers what you can do for them, not what you cannot do. For example, if you cannot deliver the material this week, but you can next week, emphasize the latter: "We can deliver next week."

Here is a list of combinations that you can use to change the subject in a positive way to what you want, putting you in control of the conversation. First, make a positive comment on what was said, pause slightly and then make a lead-in phrase, question or statement.

1. I agree, (name). Let's go over the highlights of...
2. That's definitely important, (name). What do you think about...?
3. I know what you're saying, (name). How do you feel about...?
4. Interesting, (name). Along that same line,...
5. That's great, (name). By the way, were you aware...?
6. I agree, (name). It's interesting, too, that...
7. I didn't know that, (name). I think you'll find this interesting.
8. Me, too, (name). Come to think of it, you may want to know...
9. Very good, (name). By the way, do you have any questions so far?
10. Good thought, (name). Let's look at some points on...
11. I see what you mean, (name). Might I mention that...
12. That's terrific, (name). Say, while we're on the subject, might I mention that you still have a chance to get in on...
13. Good point, (name). Let me ask you this...

Pronunciation

A dictionary is a necessity at every telemarketing station. Not only does it give the meanings of words, but also the correct pronunciations. In telemarketing, correct pronunciation is vital. People are conditioned to hear words pronounced in certain ways. At the worst, people will think you do not really know what you are talking about if you mispronounce words. At the least, people are distracted, which can be disastrous. If a TSR says something important, yet mispronounces a word or name, the listener's concentration is broken. In a routine conversation, people say, "Would you mind repeating that, please?" In telemarketing, however, a prospect/customer who has lost concentration has lost interest, and probably *will not bother to ask* you to repeat the information.

If a word or name is mispronounced throughout a presentation, the sale could be lost. It is especially harmful to mispronounce the prospect/customer's name. The frequent, *correct* use of a person's name is an effective way to maintain that person's attention in a positive way. The opposite is true if you mispronounce the name. You risk losing that positive attention. Always determine the correct pronunciation of the prospect/customer's name.

Correct pronunciation involves selecting the proper vowel and consonant sounds and stressing the proper syllables. Listed below are reminders for avoiding several common pronunciation errors.

- ACCENT THE RIGHT SYLLABLE: In the words *preferable*, *comparable*, and *abdomen*, for instance, the accent belongs on the first syllable (PREF-er-a-ble, COM-par-a-ble, AB-do-men), yet many people accent the second.

- DO NOT OMIT SOUNDS OR PASS OVER THEM TOO LIGHTLY: Notice such sounds as the first *r* in *library*, which is frequently dropped, but should be pronounced.

- DO NOT SUBSTITUTE SOUNDS: Be careful not to make substitutions such as *b* for *p* in *Baptist* or *w* for *wh* in *why*.

- DO NOT REVERSE SOUNDS: Do not say *prespiration* for *perspiration*, for example.

- DO NOT ADD SOUNDS: Do not add *r* to *idea*, so that it becomes *idear*, or *y* to *column*, so that it becomes *colyumn*.

Articulation

Good *articulation* is essential for TSRs. That is, their speech should be clearly enunciated, easily understandable and have a melodic flow. As you practice your articulation, you will want to have some idea of how speech is produced.

The Formation of Speech

In humans, the breathing system is also the speech-producing system. Air passes through the **pharynx**, a double-duty passageway shared by the eating system. The pharynx is connected to both the **esophagus** or food pipe, and the **trachea**, the air pipe leading to the lungs. At the top of the trachea is the **larynx**, the human voice box. The folds of tissue that close the larynx are the **vocal cords**. When stretched tight, they vibrate, producing sound waves in the air from the lungs. As sound from the larynx travels through the mouth, it is modified by the lips, tongue, teeth and jaws.

The sounds of speech include vowels and consonants. The *vowels* are *a, e, i, o,* and *u*. Vowel sounds are relatively unobstructed by tongue, teeth or lips. They are part of every word. When you say the vowel sounds, the air passing freely through the opening gives carrying power to your words.

Here is a list of negative phrases to avoid, and positive phrases to replace them.

Negative Words	Positive Alternatives
Don't forget to...	Please remember to...
Hold on a minute, I have to pull your file.	Would you please hold for a minute so I can... (When you come back say, "Thank you for holding.")
I don't know...	I'm not familiar with...
My advice to you is...	I recommend
	May I suggest...?
	My suggestion would be
	May I mention
	May I encourage you to
What's the problem?	Please share your concerns with me.
	Let's look the situation over.
	Please fill me in on the...
I'd like to get together.	Could we get together?
What I'd like you to do.	I'd appreciate...
	Would you consider?
We regret that we can't...	While we are unable to...we would be pleased/happy to...
We don't have that in stock.	Although we don't have that in stock, ...might work for you.
Before we..., we must have your...	So that we can..., may we have your...?

The *consonants* are all the other letters of the alphabet—all sounds produced by temporarily blocking the flow of air from the lungs. If you do not say these sounds clearly, your speech will be indistinct. It will sound careless, and may irritate or confuse the listener. It is especially important to say your consonants clearly.

For instance, as noted in the box on page 149, many people pronounce the word "picture" as "PIT-shur." This is because to pronounce it correctly, the tongue must go from the back of the mouth, where the *k* sound is made, to the front, where the *t* sound is made, very rapidly. In everyday speech people often drop the *k*, to save the effort of enunciating different sounds so close together.

You do not have to think, "Now I must put my tongue at the back of my throat so as to make the word 'picture' properly." In fact, if you did, you would probably end up like the centipede who, when someone asked how he could walk without tripping over his own feet, became so confused thinking about it that he did just that.

Producing speech sounds is something we normally do without being aware of the exact motions we are going through. Good articulation can be achieved without knowing where your tongue moves to make different sounds, but this knowledge can help you improve your speaking skills.

Equally important is concentrating on what you are saying and deciding to speak clearly. Think about enunciating properly as you speak; make a conscious effort to speak well, and keep in mind the rules you have read in this chapter. If you do, your words will be both clear and distinct.

Saying Each Sound

While it is important to say each sound clearly and distinctly, it is also important not to sound artificial. Sometimes saying sounds very distinctly can sound artificial, particularly over the telephone. Speak naturally into the mouthpiece; do not accentuate sounds in an effort to say them distinctly. You want your conversation to sound friendly and informal.

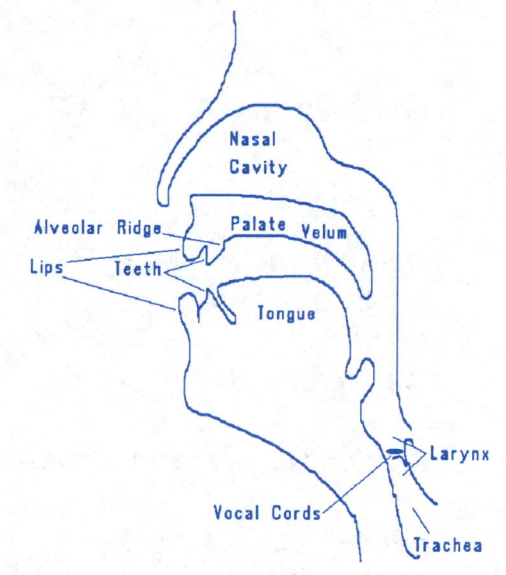

Vowels are formed by air flowing freely through the mouth, shaped by the tongue and lips.

Skipping or slurring over sounds produces especially sloppy enunciation and can be irritating to the listener. Shown below are a dozen words in which people too often skip or slur the sounds. Notice how to say those words, and how not to say them.

WORD	SAY	DO NOT SAY
ask	ASK	AX
facts	FAKTS	FAKS
adopts	a-DAHPTS	a-DAHPS
help	HELP	HEP
give me	GIV-me	GIM-me
didn't	DID-nt	DINT
didn't you	DIDnt you	DIN-SHA
going to	GO-ing to	GUNNA
want to	WANT to	WAHNA
slept	SLEPT	SLEP
picture	PIK-ture	PIT-SHUR

Suppose, for instance, that you want to tell your prospect/customer that your product or service will provide a "distinct advantage." Try pronouncing the phrase "distinct advantage," speaking each consonant as clearly as possible. Then try it again, but this time pronounce certain consonants lightly—the two t's in distinct, and the d, t, and g in advantage. Note how much more natural and conversational the words sound. Being careful to say the consonants clearly, yet not too distinctly, is an art that requires practice.

Vocabulary

Articulation
Connotation
Context
Enunciation
Esophagus
Evocative
Larynx
Pharynx
Pronunciation
Subliminal
Superlative
Trachea
Vocal Cords

Discussion Questions

1. Give examples of how such simple words as "old" and "young," "easy" and

"difficult," "large" and "small" can mean different things to different people.

2. How does being specific help a TSR?

3. Why is striking a balance between specific, detailed words and descriptive words important?

4. Explain the sentence:"The meaning of a word is not just in the word itself, it is in how and when the word is used—the context." Give an example.

5. What is meant by the statement that words have connotations?

6. List six useful categories for grouping words according to their desired or undesired psychological impact.

7. What is the difference between pronunciation and articulation? Give examples.

8. In the text there are five rules of thumb for correct pronunciation. List them and give examples for three of the five.

9. How can people improve their enunciation? Should they pay careful attention to exact tongue placement?

10. Is it possible to say words too distinctly?

Activities

This activity will help you develop your telephone fluency. The first part (A) encourages you to discover ways of describing things that will interest the prospect/customer. The second (B) exercises your positive thinking skills by asking you to find ways to change negative expressions to positive ones. The next two parts (C and D) will help you analyze the pronunciation and enunciation of well-trained speakers and to listen to and improve your own.

A. Using Descriptive Words

Think of as many colorful, descriptive words that you can to describe the objects below. Relax and have fun doing this. As you will read later, when you are relaxed your mind works more effectively. Pretend you are trying to convince someone to buy or try the item.

Compact disk player	House
Video cassette player	Swimsuit
A vacation spot	Dress or suit
Restaurant you enjoy	Can opener
A new soft drink	A movie

B. Using Positive Language

As you read, it is possible to state most facts in a positive way, even ones that are essentially negative. An example given in the text was the fact that a company was out of stock. Instead of saying it negatively, a TSR can add additional information and make it positive: stock will be available next week. Consider the negative statements below. By rewording or adding realistic additional information, make them all positive, desirable statements.

1. I only have a week to do this.

2. The sale ends Friday.

3. There is a penalty for late payments made after 30 days.

4. The day will be partly cloudy.

5. This is a cheap suit.

6. These are costly unless you buy large amounts.

7. You can't get there in under three hours.

8. I missed 3 out of 10.

9. The warranty is good for only one year.

10. There are only two grades to select from.

11. We do not deliver on Tuesdays.

12. If you are not gainfully employed, you cannot open a charge account with us.

13. You cannot get insurance coverage unless you pass the physical.

14. The guarantee does not cover anything except the manufacturing quality.

C. Speaking Professionally

Watch a television news program, and pay attention to the newscaster's pronunciation and articulation. Television newscasters are often trained actors who practice speech carefully. They sound natural, but in fact they concentrate on articulating words very distinctly and on proper pronunciation. Take notes on what you hear, on what you think the newscaster is doing to sound both clear and natural.

D. Pronouncing and Articulating

Tape record an ordinary telephone conversation with a friend. Listen for pronunciation and articulation. Transcribe the conversation and read the transcription, concentrating on pronunciation and articulation. Do some things sound sloppy or stilted? Practice until your pronunciation is correct, your enunciation clear, your sound natural.

Soft Sell vs. Hard Sell

Conversational vs. Formal

Vocabulary

Discussion Questions

Activities

Chapter 9

Creating Your Own Style

Upon completion of this chapter, you will be able to

- differentiate between soft sell and hard sell approaches,
- identify at least 10 specific soft sell techniques,
- distinguish between conversational and formal styles,
- develop a comfortable, individual style of speaking.

The right words are very important when you are describing a product or service. Equally important is the style with which you present your ideas. Your style can be reflected in many subtle ways, particularly in some of the little words you use to introduce your main thoughts. This chapter will focus on two important aspects of style—soft sell language and conversational language.

You want to develop a non-pressure, soft sell style. To do that, you must be aware of soft sell vs. hard sell words—put another way, of the difference between *non-pressure* and *pressure* words. Hard sell words direct or command someone to do something; they are pushy and badgering. Soft sell words invite people to take action; they are suggestive and agreeable. In this chapter you will see how some seemingly innocent, harmless words can cause you to project the wrong image, while the right soft sell words can make your listener receptive to your message.

Books on selling and marketing have taught for years that "people do not want to be sold, they want to buy." Yet these same books frequently then go on to suggest pressure words to use.

Think of times when you:

- bought from a high-pressure salesperson and were dissatisfied with the product/service;

- bought from a high-pressure salesperson and were upset with yourself for letting that person hoodwink you;

- were uncomfortable with a salesperson who used high-pressure words that pulled and pulled at you.

The use of hard sell, high pressure words can give your company and the telemarketing industry a bad—and undeserved—reputation. Responsible firms that are proud of their reputations do not use high-handed tactics in telemarketing. Rather, they use a soft sell approach that allows the prospect/customer to make decisions comfortably. This is the ethical approach.

Soft Sell vs. Hard Sell

Pressure words give people the uncomfortable feeling that they are being ordered to buy. In telemarketing, the pressure is even stronger than when face-to-face. That is because without the sense of sight, people automatically compensate by listening harder. Therefore, they feel the pressure of the words even more strongly.

In the sections that follow you will find some of the more commonly used thoughts and expressions in telemarketing. As you will read, most of the thoughts can be expressed in either soft sell or hard sell words. Both versions are given. Note carefully the differences and the explanations of why some words are soft sell while others are hard.

As you read these sections, think about the expressions you use naturally. You may discover that you are in the habit of using hard sell words. They may sound normal to you, and yet have a negative impact on others, especially those who do not know you well. If so, you may want to change your speech habits. Some people who, in effect, use hard sell words often in their conversation gain a reputation for being bossy or pushy when they really do not intend to be. Their reputation is based on the impression their words make, not on what they intend. In telemarketing your success is directly related to the impression that your words make. Most thoughts can be expressed in soft sell words or hard sell words. Strive to select soft sell words to make your points.

Talk To vs. Talk With

Routine-sounding phrases can contain hard sell words. For instance, you might, without thinking, say you will "talk TO" someone. But "talk TO" subtly implies talking down to someone, putting that person on a lower level.

It is better to say "talk WITH" a person, because "talking WITH" indicates friendliness, togetherness, a conversation between equals.

I Will Call vs. I'll Be Giving A Call

If you say to someone, "I WILL call you," you indicate that your mind is already made up, and that the listener has no choice.

If you say, "I'LL BE GIVING you a call, you will be using a word—GIVING—that people have been programmed to consider good. It is a word that elicits a positive response.

Tell vs. Let You Know

If you say that you will call to TELL a person something, you are using a word that takes people back to the times of their childhoods when their parents repeatedly used such phrases as, "Let me TELL you something," and, "If I have to TELL you again, I'll...." The word TELL can trigger a defensive reaction.

Instead, say, "I'll be giving you a call TO LET YOU KNOW about...." For then you will convey that you are letting the prospect/customer in on a secret, a scoop, something special.

Inform You vs. Share Some Ideas

Avoid saying, "I'm calling TO INFORM YOU," for that implies that you want to teach something to the poor, dumb listener.

A better choice is, "I'm calling TO SHARE SOME IDEAS." People have been taught since childhood that TO SHARE is good.

See If You're In The Market vs. Touch Base

When you are arranging to make a future contact, it is not helpful to say something like, "May I call again in three months TO SEE WHETHER YOU'RE IN THE MARKET then?" That approach makes people feel pressured and uncomfortable, even if it is entirely likely that they will need your product or service in three months. All they will think of is that they do not need the product or service right now.

Better simply to ask, "May I give you a call in three months or so just TO TOUCH BASE?" That soft sell approach is almost never turned down, and it opens many doors.

What I... vs Let's

When you say, "WHAT I WANT TO DO...," the listener's subconscious is likely to scream, "I don't care what this person wants; it's what I want that counts." And when you say, "WHAT I AM GOING TO DO is...," you risk sounding dictatorial, like a royal personage addressing lowly subjects.

Avoid such hard sell words. Use the soft sell, LET's. When you say, "LET's go over this...," "LET's do this..." you make the listener part of a mutually agreed upon decision. People have positive feelings when they are part of the process.

What You Must Do vs. What You Might Want To Do

When you say to someone, "This is WHAT YOU MUST DO . . ." ("what you have to do" or "what you need to do"), you set off negative reactions. The person thinks, "I don't HAVE to do anything. Who are you to tell me what I must do?"

You are more effective when you make suggestions, such as "WHAT YOU MIGHT WANT TO DO IS . . .," or "Perhaps you may want to . . .," or "Might I suggest that . . .?" These soft sell suggestions allow for a choice; no pressure is applied, and the decision is up to the prospect/customer.

Allows vs. Makes It Possible

It is unwise to say that a product or service ALLOWS the prospect/customer to do something, for ALLOW suggests that permission is required. Adults resent having to get permission to do something.

You will obtain better results when you say that a product or service MAKES IT POSSIBLE to do something, for you will be using words that indicate that doors are being opened. Everyone responds favorably to having doors opened.

Change Your Mind vs. Reach Another Conclusion

You face a touchy situation when you impart information that might make people change their minds. Generally people are admired for sticking with decisions. When people change their minds, they can lose face. The challenge is to give people the opportunity to change their minds without feeling wishy-washy.

If they have decided not to try a particular product or service, for instance, you want to give them a graceful way to reconsider. Avoid saying, "Here is some information that will MAKE YOU CHANGE YOUR MIND." Instead, say, "Here is some new information; perhaps you MIGHT REACH ANOTHER DECISION." Or, "You MIGHT DRAW ANOTHER CONCLUSION."

Scheduling Appointments vs. Arranging and Meeting

Do not say to a prospect/customer that you wish to SCHEDULE an APPOINTMENT. The word APPOINTMENT makes people think of an appointment with a dentist, to have a tooth pulled, or with a lawyer, to face being sued. The word SCHEDULE simply reminds most people of how busy they already are; they react negatively to adding to a full calendar.

Instead suggest ARRANGING a time to MEET or get together, to drop by or to stop over. Such suggestions are inviting rather than pressuring.

Conversational vs. Formal

Language can be either formal—"We request that you respond." or informal, conversational—"Please give us a call." Formal language is appropriate to written material, such as business letters, official reports and legal contracts. Except when giving a speech, which a TSR will not want to do, formal language is not what people use when talking with one another. Formal language is not appropriate for soft sell telemarketing, for it is not language that would make a prospect/customer comfortable and receptive.

Using formal language when you speak means avoiding contractions, speaking in complete sentences, and being grammatically correct. **Contractions** are two words combined into one. They are very common and you use them all the time: *I will = I'll*; *let us = let's*; *you are = you're*. No one speaks formally in natural, everyday conversation. People use contractions, speak in incomplete sentences, and often ignore strict rules of grammar. Those few who do speak formally all the time sound stuffy or snobbish to most ears.

You have a unique conversational style, based on such factors as where you grew up, your education, how your family talked, how your teachers and childhood friends talked, and what you hear from friends, coworkers and others that you deal with now. This section will help you to recognize your own style and to use it effectively in your telephone conversations with prospects/customers. You will see how you can adjust your style for certain situations, how to include particular words that enhance a positive, informal style, and how to avoid careless usages that would detract from your effectiveness.

Recognize Your Own Style

Pay attention to the words that you and others use. Notice how stuffy it sounds when someone says, "We will commence now." Note how differently you respond to, "Let's start now." Think about whether you are choosing the best words, and note words that others use that might fit your style, your approach.

As a rule the shorter, more common word is always the best one to use. We do not impress prospects/customers by using big words. For example, what is your reaction to someone who says "indubi-

---

What happens when you arbitrarily replace your own style with one that is not comfortable for you—or for your prospect/customer?

Consider the case of a woman, a leading salesperson throughout her 11-year selling career in a small town, who moved to a sizeable city. She was eager to adapt to her new environment, for she saw the opportunity to continue and even expand upon her successful sales work.

She noticed immediately that things were a bit different in the big city. For instance, suits were everywhere. The newcomer replaced her own more casual clothes with appropriate dress. She began listening to and jotting down words that the successful salespeople in her office used when making appointments, and soon revamped her own vocabulary to be more businesslike, more citified.

Disaster resulted. The woman who had always found appointment securing to be one of her strongest skills, now found she could make almost no appointments. Her boss took her aside and said if her performance did not improve, she would be fired.

Understandably distressed, the woman sat down and thought about what she was doing. She had had no trouble arranging appointments before; what was different now?

She remembered how she had once used her own approach—an approach less businesslike than her officemates, perhaps, but an approach that was personal and effective.

The prospect of being fired loomed; she felt she had nothing to lose, so she went back to using her own comfortable language, her own style of delivery. The result was an immediate turnaround. The woman began arranging appointments and making sales. Soon she was one of the top salespeople in the city office.

tably" for "without doubt"—or even "undoubtedly"? How would you react to someone who talks about her "domicile" and means her "home"? Take the common, everyday words; avoid the big words.

Adjust Your Style For Your Audience

What is conversational to one person might be stiff and uncomfortable to another. Just as you might choose different musical selections for different audiences, you can choose the right words and phrases for each audience.

This is a continuation and amplification of the rule that you will want to avoid the big, obscure word. While maintaining your own basic style, you adapt it for the audience you are talking with. For example, you might take a chatty approach to a homeowner who indicates she or he has time and is interested in talking. On the other hand, if you are calling a busy executive of a large company, you will be polite, but brief and to the point—certainly not chatty.

Use Contractions

Use contractions naturally. Contractions have an easy, flowing, informal sound that is important to the soft sell approach.

For example, say these words and listen to the difference.

I am	*I'm*
You are	*You're*
We will	*We'll*
They are	*They're*
Let us	*Let's*

Avoid Irritating Words

While contractions add to the naturalness and comfort of a telephone conversation, slang does not. In general, slang is irritating; using it detracts from your presentation. Stay away from such careless replies as "Yeah," "Yep," or "Uh-huh." What you want to say is "Yes." Being informal does not mean being sloppy in your speech. Nor does the fact that informal speech does not follow all the rules of formal grammar mean that you are free to make errors.

It is important not to use words or contractions that are not recognized as acceptable. A contraction such as "ain't," for example, is to be avoided, as are slang words, swear words, or words with questionable connotations.

Use Words That Sound Positive

Some words with particularly positive connotations can fit easily and naturally into an informal, conversational approach. Listed here are some words that have positive connotations according to a study by the psychology department of a major university. You can add to your effectiveness when you use such words with a prospect/customer.

Discovery	Money
Guarantee	Safety
Health	Proven
(P/C's Name)	Love
You	Results
New	Free
Save	Special
Easy	Help

Vocabulary

Contractions

Discussion Questions

1. Explain the difference between hard sell and soft sell words.

2. Why does the routine-sounding phrase "talk to you" have a negative effect in telemarketing? Discuss alternatives. How are they more effective?

3. Why do such seemingly natural phrases as "I will call you" and "I'll tell you" have a negative impact on the listener? List some alternatives, and explain why they work better.

4. Why is it important to avoid saying "What I want" or "What I'd like" or "What I am going to do"? What are some other ways of saying the same thing?

5. What is formal language used for? What about informal? Which do you as a TSR try to use? Why?

6. Why is it important for you to use the style of speech with which you are comfortable? What determines that style?

7. Some people think it is important to use big words when speaking with people, in order to impress them. Is this true for telemarketing? Explain.

8. For the most part, as you have read, it is important to maintain an informal tone in telemarketing conversations. Where do you draw the line? Explain.

Activities

These exercises are designed to give you an awareness of soft sell and hard sell words, to help you think of soft sell words that you can use to stimulate positive ideas in the prospect's mind, and to help you create your own conversational style as a TSR.

A. Differentiate Between Hard and Soft Sell

Television commercials are not like TSRs because they only talk at people who cannot respond. In some ways they are similar to the persuasion step of a telesales dialog, in that they are aimed at selling a service or product by giving features and benefits. For two or three nights, keep notes as you listen to the commercials. Listen for the use of any of the soft or hard sell words. Jot down the hard sell ones that you hear. Then, later, write alternate choices of soft sell words that you could use to sell the same product or service. See if you hear any soft sell ones you would like to add to your collection.

As you listen to the commercials, think of your reaction. How do you react to hard sell? How do you react to soft sell? Record your reactions with enough information about the commercial so that you can discuss them in class.

B. Use Soft Sell Techniques

Work in small groups. Pick a topic that everyone in the group is comfortable with—preferably something to do with telesales, such as a particular product/service. Working on your own, prepare a short telephone dialog in your own comfortable language. Pick a partner and take turns role playing your dialog before the group, and making notes on the way each individual chooses to describe the same subject. If you like, tape yourself speaking so you can listen again when you are finished.

We often use hard sell words and phrases without being aware of it. After listening to your tape, review the words and phrases you listed. Study them to develop an awareness of your use. This will begin triggering a soft sell response to replace the hard sell one.

Make a note of words others use that mean the same as yours. You might want to add them to your vocabulary or just remember them for the discussion. Listen for the words that appeal to people. You may want to start a collection of words you feel are effective and keep them for reference.

C. Develop Your Own Style

Besides using soft sell language, you want to speak in a way that is natural and comfortable for you. This exercise will help you identify your own style and find words and expressions to suit.

Write down your partner's presentation from exercise A. Read it aloud. Do the soft sell words your partner chose feel comfortable to you? If not, what would you replace them with? Make a note of soft sell words and phrases that fit your personality best.

Now practice a telephone dialog with your partner using the words that you find most comfortable. Since these words are especially important in the subtle, less obvious places, try using them in the transitions between steps of a sale: from opening to fact finding, from fact finding to persuading, and from persuading to closing. Does the use of conversational language make the flow of the conversation easier?

Unit IV
TELEPHONE DELIVERY SKILLS

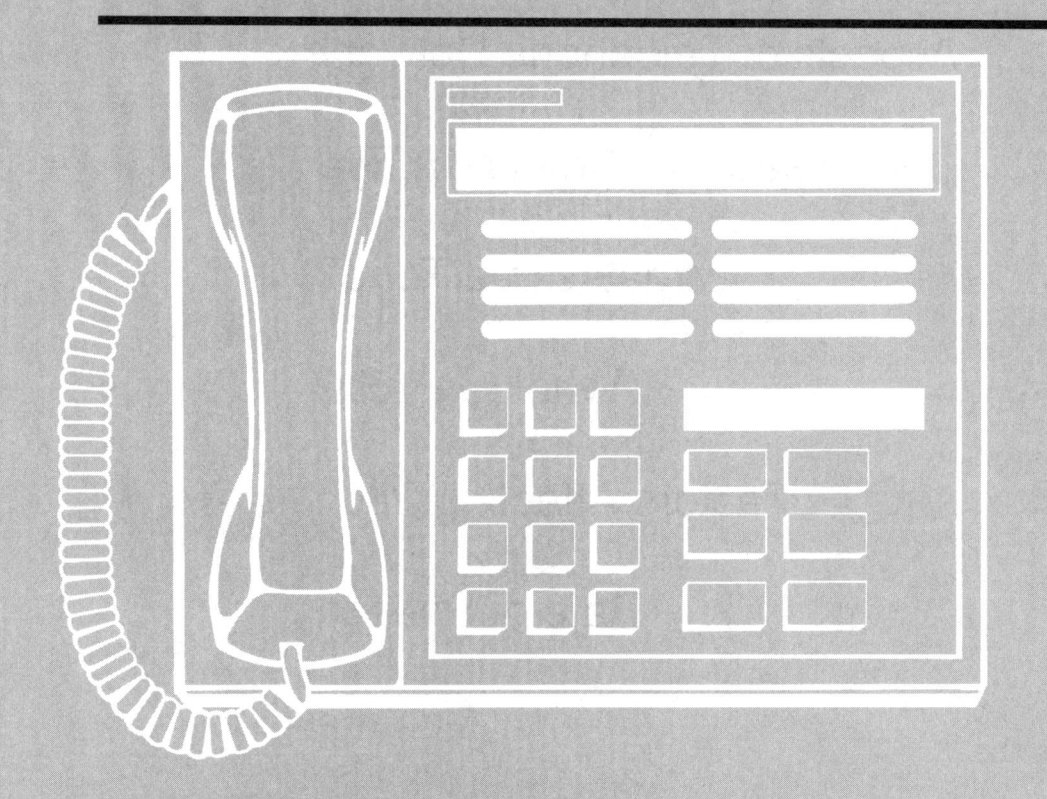

Chapter 10—Establishing Your Tone

Chapter 11—Adding Zest to Your Voice

Chapter 12—Listening to Communicate

Lacking Visual Clues

Aspects of Telephone Delivery

Reaching the Mind's Eye

What Is in a Tone?

What Is Pitch?

Factors Affecting Pitch

Rate of Speech

Volume

Vocabulary

Discussion Questions

Activities

Chapter 10

Establishing Your Tone

Upon completion of this chapter, you will be able to

- use vocal skills to compensate for the absence of visual clues,
- identify seven important vocal qualities, and four aspects of delivery that influence them,
- use five factors to control pitch,
- identify two misconceptions about rate of speech,
- recognize three factors affecting volume.

On the telephone, words are all you have to achieve your objectives. Consider, however, that in face-to-face selling, choice of words accounts for only 7 percent of people's success, the sound of their voice accounts for 38 percent, and their body language, 55 percent, according to a study by Dr. Alfred Mehrabian, UCLA.

In telephone communications, obviously, body language, the major influence on success, is not a factor. Does that mean TSRs face a nearly impossible situation? No. TSRs learn to use their voice quality to compensate for the absence of body language.

Listening, always crucial to effective communication, also becomes more important in telephone conversations. In Chapter 12 you will learn about developing listening skills. In this chapter, you will concentrate on using your voice to make up for that missing body language.

Lacking Visual Clues

Dr. Mehrabian's study shows how much people rely on body language—a visual element—in communication. The study suggests why many people may dislike making or receiving telemarketing calls. When using a telephone and thus lacking visual clues, both the caller and the person being called may find themselves outside of their "comfort zones." They are more likely to experience negative feelings, like fear of the unknown. The study makes clear that TSRs have to compensate for the lack of body language, the lack of visual feedback.

Compensating for the missing visual contact, and keeping a "human touch," is an important element of the soft sell approach to telemarketing. By developing your telephone delivery skills—that is, by becoming aware of the qualities of your voice and working carefully to improve those qualities—you will learn that you can be effective without the visual element, because your voice quality will compensate for it.

Use Body Language

Despite the lack of visual clues, you can use your body language while speaking on the phone. Even though your listener, the prospect/customer, cannot see your body language, using body language can affect how you sound. Your posture, expressions, and gestures are all part of your natural way of speaking. Use them when talking on the telephone to help yourself sound comfortable and enthusiastic rather than uncomfortable or listless.

Use Gestures

Gestures can also clear your thinking and give direction to your thoughts. For instance, they can stimulate you to think of more descriptive words and to place emphasis on strategic words and phrases. You may be gesturing to indicate that something is tiny and delicate, or waving your arm to emphasize that something is huge. These gestures can serve to animate your voice and also to make you think of ways to express those ideas with your voice.

Aspects of Telephone Delivery

The box on this page lists seven characteristics of the voice of a good TSR. To give your own voice these characteristics, consider the different aspects that affect it. Several aspects affect how you sound. These aspects include tone, pitch, rate, and volume.

For example, using volume, pauses and inflection, you can add emphasis to what you are saying on the telephone, much as a person in face-to-face conversation will use a gesture to do so. (You will read about pitch, rate, and volume later in this chapter.)

Use Your Own Voice

Keep in mind that your goal is to make changes that suit your own style, your own personality—not to develop a whole new personality style. Trying to create a different telephone personality would harm your efforts, decreasing your productivity and sales.

You have a unique body structure and personality; your pitch, tone, inflection, and choice of words are unique to you. In developing your telephone delivery, you will not be making changes that do not fit you, but rather finding what is best — natural—for you.

Maximize Results

It takes effort and practice to use your voice most effectively, and you do not want to waste that effort—or diminish your effectiveness as a TSR—with distracting noises that are not, or need not be, part of your delivery. Remember what you read in Chapter 5 about avoid-

> Voice quality is one of your most important tools. A good TSR has a voice that is:
> - strong and easily heard
> - relaxed and natural
> - confident
> - energetic and enthusiastic
> - never rushed or impatient
> - interesting and caring
> - using inflections and pauses that give it melodic rhythm

ing unnecessary noises, such as clicking your pen, that can form a distracting background to your telephone conversation.

You might want to review Unit III, "Telephone Fluency," as you begin this unit on telephone delivery. Combining the right words—especially non-pressure, soft sell words—with appealing voice qualities will help make you a successful TSR.

Reaching the Mind's Eye

Although in telemarketing you have no actual visual contact, you can use your voice to send a message to what you might call the "third eye" that every human possesses—the "mind's eye." Face-to-face salespeople also want to reach the mind's eye; however, they rely more on the prospect/customer looking at the product or observing them because that is more familiar to them.

In a sense, TSRs have an advantage here. When sight is eliminated, as it is over the phone, people automatically compensate for that loss. Their mind's eye becomes keener and forms clearer images of the data it receives. As a TSR, you can take advantage of this heightened sense by making sure that your words and voice create positive images in the mind's eye of the prospect/client.

You want your words and voice to be stimulating, to generate excitement and desire for the product/service. You want the prospect/customer, in his or her mind's eye, to imagine using and enjoying the product/service. For that to happen, you need not only choose clear, descriptive words, but also have a pleasant, positive tone to your voice.

What Is in a Tone?

Tone is the emotional quality of a person's voice. Tone conveys feelings and attitudes; it indicates whether the speaker is pleased or upset, enthusiastic or weary, friendly or hostile.

For example, when you were a child, you could tell by the tone of your mother's voice when she called your name whether you had better hop to or could dally around a bit longer. And think how often you hear someone say something like, "Watch out for Sam today. I can tell by the tone of his voice that he's in a bad mood."

In the same way, your prospects/clients can detect your feelings just by listening to your tone. They detect your general alertness, your enthusiasm for your job, your confidence in yourself and in your product/service. They also can detect listlessness, lack of interest or knowledge, discontent, and irritation.

Why Tone is Important

On the telephone, your *voice* is not only *you*; your *voice* is also the *company*. You want your tone to project your enthusiasm for your product/service and your interest in the person with whom you are speaking.

Value of a Smile

You may not realize it, but how you shape the borders of your mouth will affect the tone of your voice. When you smile, you create a tone that is pleasant and positive. By smiling, you can convey friendliness rather than a "strictly business" approach, enthusiasm rather than boredom, energy rather than fatigue, and interest in the listener rather than "I'm just doing my job."

The simple act of smiling as you speak can have a profound impact on your tone, and therefore on the image you project.

Even if you are having a bad day—worried about a sick relative, annoyed over traffic jams—a cheerful tone is vital for effective telemarketing. Consciously putting a smile on your face will help you to keep your tone free of the effects of negative distractions.

When you smile, you sound more cheerful, pleasant, and more confident. In telemarketing, you want to convey your confidence in your talents, skills, and knowledge. You especially want people to know that you have complete confidence in your product/service.

Even when you are new to telemarketing, and may not feel quite confident in yourself, you can be convincing to the prospect/customer—and even succeed at convincing yourself—by making a conscious effort to smile as you speak into the telephone. The effect is a bit like that in the song from the classic musical, *The King and I*, which goes like this: "Whenever I feel afraid, I hold my head erect, and whistle a happy tune, so no one will suspect I'm afraid." A smile on your face will put confidence in your voice, and your

> Remember, on the telephone, your *voice* is not only *you*. On the telephone, your voice is the *company*—as this example illustrates:
>
> Ann, a young mother with small children, often called ahead when she went into town to shop. To avoid unnecessarily hauling her little ones around, she liked to make sure in advance that the items she needed were available.
>
> One day when she called to the durgstore where she always shopped, the clerk who answered the telephone sounded uncordial, impatient. Perhaps the clerk was having a problem, and Ann simply called at the wrong time. But Ann did not like the tone of the clerk's voice; it made her feel that the clerk considered her a pest. "I don't have to be treated that way," Ann decided. "There's another drug store in town."
>
> Ann had been doing business for seven years with the first drug store; she had never received poor merchandise or poor service. She did not even like the other drug store very much; it was considerably smaller.
>
> Those things no longer mattered with her. Because of the clerk's unfriendly tone, she took her business elsewhere. For Ann, that voice was the company—a company she would now avoid.

prospect/customer will have reason to have confidence in you and your product/service.

Practice, of course, is important. Your voice is like a musical instrument in that regard: with practice, its tone improves.

What Is Pitch?

Pitch refers to the lowness or highness of your voice—not its loudness, or *volume*. In music, pitch is represented by the notes on the scale. As you read earlier, the sounds of your voice are made when your vocal cords vibrate. Changing the length of the vocal cords produces variations in pitch, just as placing your finger on the string of a guitar (shortening it) makes the note higher. You control these changes in vocal cord length without even thinking.

Everyone has a level of pitch at which he or she is most comfortable. At that natural level there is no strain on the vocal cords—no strain that produces harshness and mars the quality of the voice. This section will help you find your own main pitch level and the range of tones above and below that level that is comfortable for you. This knowledge is necessary for a telemarketing career because you will use your voice for long periods of time, and you will want to avoid harshness in your tones and tightness in your throat.

Comparing your voice to a musical instrument makes sense. Think of it as a valuable instrument, one that should be cared for properly. Music is written in many different keys—for example, the key of C. When using your own musical instrument—your voice—keep in mind what is natural for you, what is not a strain. Speak in a key that is natural and comfortable for you, which you might call the key of *B Natural*.

Factors Affecting Pitch

Most people have their own pitch pattern, a range of several notes. This range is where they are most comfortable, and it is determined largely by factors over which people have no control—age and sex.

- *Age*: For instance, young children have higher voices because their vocal cords have not yet developed full length and thickness. Older people experience a change in their habitual pitch pattern based on their use or abuse of their voices over the years.

- *Sex:* Whether you are male or female plays a large role in determining your voice's pitch. Men usually have larger—longer and wider—vocal folds. The larger the fold, the lower the voice. Women have shorter and thinner vocal folds. The thinner, shorter female vocal cords, however, have more flexibility.

You need not worry about the factors that are beyond your control. Other factors, however, are within your control.

When Pitch Can Be Controlled

Although people have a pitch base of several notes where they are most comfortable, some things can cause voices to go up or down several notes from what is natural and comfortable and thus can produce a pitch that is not pleasant to hear. Eating, drinking and smoking, and tension can all adversely affect your pitch.

On the other hand, smiling can improve your pitch. Pay careful attention to these factors, largely within your control, that affect your pitch.

Eating, Drinking and Smoking

Certain foods can irritate your vocal cords. For instance, dairy products create phlegm, which will cause you to keep clearing your throat while on the phone. This does not mean that you should not eat dairy products; it does mean you will want to avoid them just prior to making calls. Be aware also that:

- Foods or beverages that are extremely hot or cold can damage your vocal cords.

- Smoking severely irritates your vocal cords.

- Alcohol can give your voice a hoarse quality.

Tension

Tension causes a tight throat that produces harsh sounds of higher pitch than is right for a particular voice. It can cause serious problems for TSRs and cannot be ignored. Given the nature of their work—making continuing calls, encountering all kinds of people, and having to be productive—TSRs are subject to tension.

How Tension Can Be Reduced

Tension will always tighten the muscles of the neck, reduce the size of the air passageway, and give the vocal cords less room to vibrate. A tense TSR cannot speak naturally, and so it is important to learn ways to reduce stress and tension and increase productivity. Here are some simple techniques you can use to reduce tension.

Take Breaks

TSRs make many, many contacts in any given day. Outside salespeople have unwinding time between calls—driving, parking, walking, and waiting. Although they are also under pressure, they are not under the gun hour after hour, dialed number after dialed number. They have a change of scene, sometimes the physical exercise of walking, a period of time between calls to rest their minds and rejuvenate them before their next contact.

TSRs, who do not go out driving and walking, should use the tension-relieving 55/5 system. That is, they are on the phone no longer than 55 minutes without a break. Their hourly, five-minute breaks—which are necessary to their productivity—should be in addition to normal company breaks.

The five-minute breaks are vital because of the adrenaline buildup that takes place during calls. The flow of adrenaline is a marvelous thing when someone needs to flee from a dangerous situation. But in the daily life of a TSR, who experiences some stress and is physically inactive, adrenaline simply accumulates in the muscles hour after hour. The human body has no system for the elimination of excess adrenaline; exercise is the only way the body can get rid of it.

The longer TSRs sit without moving about, the tighter their muscles become, especially in the shoulders and neck. As these muscles become tighter, they force the bones out of alignment. As a result fatigue, headaches, and upper and lower backache can occur if precautions are not taken. A person experiencing this kind of discomfort cannot work at peak levels. Taking a break, getting up and walking around, stretching, all help to reduce the level of adrenaline and loosen stiff muscles. So even though phoning time is shorter because of these breaks, more and more companies are realizing they are well worth it because productivity improves.

Change Positions

TSRs can relieve tension by alternating sitting and standing while phoning. Many TSRs like to have a folding desktop shelf added at a height comfortable for standing, to ease back muscles.

In the activities at the end of this chapter, you will find more techniques to help relieve tension on the job.

Use a Headset

Using a headset helps make standing possible, leaves the hands free for note taking and data entry, and it helps reduce neck problems caused by tense muscles. You will feel your neck muscles tense if you try using your shoulder to hold a phone to your ear. If you hold the phone on your left side, for instance, the muscles are elongated on the right side and shortened on the left, and can hurt during calling (and also afterward, as the muscles are stretched back into shape).

Using a headset brings not only more comfort, but also better voice quality. Remember, sound is created by vibration of the vocal cords. When your neck is bent, the air passageway is bent also, cutting the air flow and giving your vocal cords less space in which to vibrate. The result is a poor, tense voice quality.

Also, when you hold a phone on your shoulder, the mouthpiece tends to slip under your chin as you move, and you are not speaking directly into the phone. Your voice quality will be poor, and your prospect/customer will have to strain to understand you. When prospects/customers have to strain to hear, they lose their attention and interest, which leads to lost sales.

Rate of Speech

Two common misconceptions about rate of telephone speech are:

- You need to speak more slowly than normal over the phone to make certain that you are heard.

- You need to speak more slowly over the phone so the listener has time to grasp the meaning of what you say.

Both of these ideas are wrong. Older equipment sometimes caused problems; the occasional poor connection does occur. In general, people can actually hear and understand *more clearly* over the phone than face-to-face because:

- There are no distractions caused by visual images as there are in a face-to-face conversation.

- There is amplification in the telephone that makes the sound clear.

- The two people interacting are not seated several feet apart, they are actually mouth-to-ear. It is hardly possible to get much closer than that for clarity.

These circumstances make it unnecessary to slow down for clarity.

Use a Conversational Rate

The phone in no way distorts the thinking process; people do not need more time to understand what they hear over the phone. Speaking slowly does not improve understanding; it discourages interest. A reason some TSRs sound as if they are reading is that they are speaking too slowly. When people speak too slowly, they lose the smooth flow tying words together. A good flow of words is the magic that makes it possible for professional TSRs to read a script, word for word, and sound as if the words are just rolling off their tongues.

Effective TSRs have a conversational rate of speech. It sounds natural because it is the rate people are used to hearing and with which they are most comfortable. When people are comfortable, their attention span increases, as does their interest. That makes it important to use a rate that people find comfortable.

In telemarketing, slowing down your normal rate can produce negative images in the mind of prospect/customers who:

- may feel that you do not sound natural,

- may think of you as reading rather than conversing,

- may feel they are being talked down to in that you are speaking slowly because you think they are not intelligent.

Conviction and belief go together with enthusiasm and excitement and usually are not expressed as effectively in slow speech.

According to Evelyn Burge Bowling, in her book *Voice Power*, a fast speaker says 190 words per minute and above, a slow speaker says 120 words or less per minute, and the ideal rate is 150 to 170 words per minute.

When a caller speaks slowly, the listener may feel annoyed: Here is someone who seems to have all the time in the world and is about to waste a lot of theirs. The listener thinks, between the words, "Why doesn't this person hurry up?"

Such negative thoughts on the part of the prospect/customer play a large role in decreased sales. Such thoughts always keep the prospect/customer from paying attention to the ideas the sales person is trying to share. The prospect/customer simply says "Not interested." and ends the conversation.

When Slowness DOES Help

There is one situation that does require you to slow down: handling complaints. People who are complaining usually speak rapidly; in fact, the more upset they are, the more rapidly they speak. If you are not careful, you may find yourself imitating their rate of speech. Since the rushed speech of a complainant conveys distress and often frustration, you obviously want to avoid imitating it.

The first step in calming down complainants is to speak slowly. That will help them slow down, for their minds will subconsciously tune into the slower rate. A slow speaking rate denotes calmness, which is catching.

In handling complaints, you want to stay in control and not allow the complainant to draw you into a fast-talking confrontation. (Remember the techniques in Chapter 7 for handling complaints.)

If You Do Feel Rushed

In avoiding the risk of speaking too slowly, be careful not to make the mistake of speaking too fast. What you want is a natural, conversational rate of speech. Occasionally, a TSR may feel rushed: there is so much information to impart, so many calls to make, so little time, it seems, for everything. This feeling comes more from within than without. The best ways to deal with it are to be well prepared and to remember breathing exercises and other tension-reducers. Do not let your feeling of being rushed cause you to speak too fast.

While speaking slowly is to be avoided, rushed speech can also cause problems. If you rush, you will not be articulating your words clearly. You may give the prospect/customer the feeling that you do not have time for him or her. Or you may sound to the prospect/customer too much like a carnival pitchman, like a fast-talking huckster who wants to make a quick sale. You do not want to create such feelings under any circumstances.

Volume

Volume refers to the noise level of your voice, as opposed to pitch, which refers to whether your voice is low or high. Voice volume can be a soft whisper in a high pitch or a loud shout in a low pitch. Your voice volume can be loud, moderate, or quiet. Usually moderate volume is best; however, a variety of factors can make your volume too loud or too quiet.

In the next sections, you will look at these factors that make it difficult for you to maintain a pleasant, moderate volume. You will see that most of these factors are within your control, and that by paying attention to them you will be better able to control your volume, which affects your overall voice quality.

Tension Affects Volume

Tension affects volume as well as other aspects of voice. When people are stressed and nervous, their throat muscles tighten, and their volume—like their pitch—can sound uncomfortable and unnatural. Consider a case of extreme stress—a person's being attacked on the street by a mugger. The victim's throat muscles immediately tense, and the victim may do one of three things:

- Give a shrill or booming yell that is much louder than his or her normal voice.

- Make a whispery, barely audible sound.

- Be unable to utter any sound at all because of extreme tightness in the throat and chest.

These, of course, are extreme examples. However, you may find at times that tension will cause you to begin speaking loudly—or more quietly than you should. You may be tense because you are trying to make too many calls, facing difficult calls, feeling unconfident, or worrying about reaching a sales goal. You will need to recognize such possibilities, deal with them, and concentrate on maintaining moderate volume. By keeping your voice at a moderate level, you are in charge of the mood of the conversation.

Following are some things you want to be sure never to do:

- Raise your voice, even when the person at the other end is raising his or her voice. This can only increase tension and hinder solutions.

- Use too quiet a voice. Such a voice can irritate and distract listeners. A too-quiet voice may also make the listener feel that you lack confidence in yourself and in your product/service.

As you learned in the section on pitch, each person has a natural speaking pitch pattern—a range of five to seven notes. When you try to speak in a pitch that is not natural for you, you will have less volume. And, if you try to speak more loudly than is natural for you, your pitch may become shrill and grating.

Level of Energy and Enthusiasm

People who are not feeling well, or who have a low level of energy and enthusiasm, will have low volume (as well as a slower rate of speech). If you are well-rested, knowledgeable about your product/service, and enjoy your work, you will be well on your way to having pleasant, moderate volume to your voice.

Mouth Size and Speech Habits

The size and movements of your mouth also affect volume. Basic mouth size is, of course, something a person is born with and cannot change. One reason that men have more volume than women is that their mouths are usually larger, and can take in more air. However, by using their mouths in various ways, people make changes in their volume. For instance:

- Little jaw movement and a closed-mouth manner of speaking produces not only unclear sounds but also low volume.

- Proper jaw movement and mouth openness contribute to moderate volume (and to clear enunciation).

- Exaggerated jaw and mouth movements produce increased volume as well as overly distinct words.

Judging Your Volume

Because you are so accustomed to your own voice, you may not be able to judge how you sound to others. You can work with your classmates to determine how you sound and what your volume is. React to what your classmates suggest and practice speaking at volumes they find most pleasing and comprehensible.

Hearing loss may cause people to speak loudly and not realize it. If you have some difficulty hearing, you will want to have your classmates listen to you and tell you how you sound, so that you can adjust your volume if necessary.

Handling Complaints

Just as slowing your rate of speech is helpful in handling complaints, so is lowering your volume. A quiet voice denotes calmness, and it will help defuse the irritation of the complainant.

Vocabulary

Tone
Pitch
Volume

Discussion Questions

1. Is body language of any use at all to TSRs? Explain your answer.

2. What are seven characteristics of the voice of a good TSR?

3. What does the phrase *reaching the mind's eye* mean for TSRs?

4. What can telephone listeners tell from the tone of your voice?

5. What does putting a smile on your face put into your voice that your prospect/customer hears?

6. How do you improve the tone of your voice for telemarketing?

7. What is *pitch*? What are the major, controllable factors that determine it?

8. Describe three steps you can take to relieve tension.

9. What are the two most common misconceptions regarding rate of speech on the telephone? Explain why they are wrong.

10. What rate and volume are appropriate for handling complaints? Why?

11. Can tension affect volume, as it affects other aspects of voice? Explain.

Activities

These activities will help you use your natural voice qualities. The first should be done in small groups. The second and third can be done alone or with the class.

A. Compensating for Lack of Visual Clues

This activity will help you use gestures and body language to overcome the lack of visual clues on the telephone. Your class can work together or break up into small groups. Either way, each of you will have a chance to give two brief talks while the others listen.

When you are the speaker, briefly describe something enjoyable—a trip, a hobby, or a movie, perhaps—while the listeners watch closely and jot down a) the tone they hear and b) the gestures, movements and expressions that they see. The listeners can then share their notes with each other and with you. Did you sound lively, interested? How did your gestures, expressions and movements contribute to the effect of the talk? Was there a moment when you smiled during your talk? Did your jaw move more when you smiled? Did your lips move more easily? What happened to your neck muscles? (Put your hand on your throat.)

Take a second turn describing something enjoyable, but this time the listeners will close their eyes during the talk. Afterward, the listeners will open their eyes and check their lists. Did you sound lively and enthusiastic? Did the listeners miss the effects of your gestures or expressions? Did you make up for their lack? Could the listeners tell whether you were smiling? How could they tell? Was it easier for them to concentrate, to tune in? What made it easier or harder for them to concentrate?

B. Controlling Pitch, Rate, and Volume

Tension, as you read, is one of the five factors affecting pitch. It also affects rate and volume. This activity will help you reduce tension. You can add other exercises that you find helpful, such as the relaxing exercises in Chapter 4.

HEAD ROLLS: Slowly move your head clockwise, concentrating on loosening and moving the neck muscles. After a few turns, go counterclockwise.

STRETCHING: Stand up, stretch your arms as high as you can, and hold for a count of 10. Then relax for a count of 10. Repeat several times.

SHOULDER ROLLS: While sitting or standing, raise both shoulders and roll them forward several times. Then roll them backwards several times.

BREATHING: Stand straight, raise your arms above your head. Breathe in deeply, hold, then breathe out, counting to five for each step.

C. Finding the Right Rate

This activity will help you find your own natural rate of speech. Give a brief talk on something familiar to you. Record two minutes of the talk. Play back the recording and transcribe it. Listen to the recording again and mark the written copy at the end of each minute. Count the number of words per minute—this is your regular rate of speech. Get comments from your classmates. Did you sound rushed? Hesitant?

Using Your Voice to Add Emphasis

Various Kinds of Emphasis

Pause to Emphasize

Inflection

Sample Script

Vocabulary

Discussion Questions

Activities

Chapter 11

Adding Zest to Your Voice

Upon completion of this chapter, you will be able to

- use at least five techniques to add emphasis to the spoken word,
- use non-verbal pauses to punctuate speech effectively,
- vary inflection for dynamic delivery.

Emphasizing, or stressing, certain syllables, words, or phrases is one way in which people convey what they mean when they talk or write. Emphasis is an important aid to understanding.

As you know, people communicate with their voices, their words, and their body language. Emphasis plays a role in all three.

Research shows that people use body language for many kinds of emphasis. They give additional meaning to what they say by the way they sit, stand, move their heads or use their hands. For instance, people might lower their heads to emphasize sadness, or hold up a hand to emphasize how high something is. But of course such forms of emphasis are not conveyed over the telephone.

With written words, emphasis is achieved not only with word choice (for instance, with superlatives like "best") and punctuation marks (like the exclamation point), but also with such devices as color, italics, underlining, highlighting, bold print, capital letters.

Using Your Voice to Add Emphasis

The written word is important to telemarketing prompters and scripts and to many operations of a telemarketing firm. In your day-to-day work as a TSR, however, you will not be using exclamation points or capital letters for emphasis. You will use your voice to add emphasis to the words and to every conversation with each prospect/customer. By using different kinds of emphasis, you will be more effective.

You can place emphasis on the spoken word by:

- slowing down or speeding up the rate of speech,
- holding the word to be emphasized for a couple of seconds, just as you would hold a note of music,
- raising or lowering volume,
- pausing before or after the word or phrase to be emphasized,
- changing pitch (which gives inflection to a sound).

Various Kinds of Emphasis

By recognizing, using and combining the various kinds of emphasis, you will make your speech more interesting and effective; you will be better able to hold the attention of your prospect/customer.

You might say a particular part of a sentence slowly. For instance, if you say, "Features of this car include," and then slowly list the individual features one by one, you will be emphasizing those features. Or, you might conclude your talk with a faster listing—a way of emphasizing how numerous those features are.

Or, you might hold one sound in a word. You might say, for instance, "It comes in *beau*-tiful shades of magenta and lavender," drawing out the *beau* slowly.

Volume can play a similar role. You add emphasis by raising your volume a bit, or lowering it a bit. A slightly louder word—"It can save *hours*"—can be effective. So can a slightly hushed phrase—"The fabric is *so soft*." You almost automatically raise your volume when you say something like, "I hear your team won," but lower it for something like, "I'm sorry to hear about your son's injury." Raising volume for emphasis is such a common practice that you want to be careful to use it sparingly.

Pause to Emphasize

Different sentence lengths and conversational phrases in a prepared telemarketing dialog or script help provide opportunities for appropriate pauses. You also need to consider the usefulness of pauses whenever you speak with a prospect/customer.

The Work of the Pause

As you have read, the voice can be considered a musical instrument. Consider the pause as the equivalent of the musical rest. In music, a *rest* is a short interval between notes. This interval can make the difference between good music and terrific music. It adds meaning to the music and gives it flair. It makes a note stand out or linger.

You can give meaning and flair to your speech by the effective use of pauses. You can also give your hard-working vocal cords a rest. And, if you are feeling rushed or nervous, pauses are a good way to slow down.

Pauses punctuate thoughts in the same way that periods, commas, and other marks punctuate the written word. They separate ideas and keep things from running together, just as periods and commas do. They add emphasis, as exclamation points do. They give the listener a feeling of anticipation for what is coming next, as a dash does.

When you use a pause for emphasis, you may place it after or before an important point.

Immediately following an important point, it will highlight the idea and give the listener a chance to think it through.

Immediately before an important point, it becomes what is sometimes called a *creative* pause. It will:

- give the listener a feeling of anticipation for what is about to be said;

- recapture the listener's attention if it is wandering.

Teachers use a version of this technique. If their students are distracted—suddenly watching action outside the classroom window, for example—experienced teachers will simply stop, and not say a word, until their pause draws the students' attention back. When the normal hum of words ceases, people notice.

Learn When to Pause

A pause is a deliberate interval of Pauses;As punctuationsilence, not a hesitation. But sometimes people are afraid to pause. They fear they will seem to be hesitating instead of pausing deliberately.

To fill what they fear will be awkward silences, people make what are called *verbalized pauses*—such sounds as "*um*," "*er*," and "*ah*;" such words as "*you know*," and "*like*." Because of their apprehension, they fill the spaces. A verbalized pause defeats all the intended results of a pause. It does not stress a point, or give the listener time for anticipation.

Verbalized pauses can, however, teach you something: where to put an effective, non-verbalized pause. Where you pause to say "Er" is probably a good spot to pause, period. Once you recognize that verbalized pauses like "um" and non-verbalized pauses come at the very same spots, you can gradually eliminate verbalized pauses and replace them with pauses.

Punctuating with pauses will help you to sound knowledgeable, confident, professional. Listeners will feel that you know what you are talking about, believe in your product/service, are not rushing them, and have an experienced, professional approach—one that merits their trust.

Inflection

Inflection is the raising or lowering of pitch at the beginning, middle, or end of a word. This change makes the voice expressive and varied. Without inflection, a voice is only a *monotone*. It stays on the same note most of the time, displays little flexibility or expression, and bores the listener.

Basically there are two kinds of inflection—upward and downward. Each conveys different meanings when used at the end of a sentence or phrase. Sometimes upward and downward inflections are both heard in the same word. These mixed inflections add life to speech.

Downward Inflection ↘

Downward Inflection is ending the word on a lower note. When you end phrases or sentences with downward inflection, you sound knowledgeable and decisive. People are comfortable buying products/services from salespeople that sound confident and knowledgeable, and so using downward inflection is an important part of a persuasive, soft sell approach. It conveys what might be called confident expectancy to your prospect/customer.

A sentence ending with a downward inflection is perceived by the listenerd as a statement even if it is a question. For example, a soft sell response to a person too busy to talk now is:

- *Since that's the case, I won't take any more of your time now. Instead, may I give you a call later today ↗, or would sometime tomorrow be better ↘?*

When the prospect/customer hears an alternate choice question converted to a statement by the use of inflection, he or she is more likely to make a choice rather than giving a no response. This is an excellent technique to use during the closing step of the sale.

Upward Inflection ↗

Ending a sentence with downward inflection is like ending it with a period. **Upward inflection**, on the other hand, punctuates a sentence with a question mark. The difference is clear between "This is important?" and "This is important." Unless you really intend to ask a question, raising the pitch at the end of a sentence conveys:

- lack of confidence
- need for approval
- inadequate knowledge
- indecisiveness

The voice is like a musical instrument, its pitch rising and falling to produce a variety of effects.

Sometimes people get into the habit of ending sentences with upward inflections. They may simply mean to sound cooperative. But if you fall into that habit, you will lose much of your effectiveness as a TSR.

Mix Your Inflections

When you use mixed inflections—upward and downward inflections within words and sentences—you avoid speaking in a monotone. For instance, when you say "Congratulations" to someone, each syllable does not have the same pitch. Lyle V. Mayer, in his book *Notebook for Voice and Diction*, notes the difference between a monotone and a voice with inflection. He describes a *voice with inflections* with such terms as:

- enthusiastic delivery,
- alive,
- alert,
- vocally animated,
- dynamic way of expressing oneself,
- lots of vocal personality,
- varied,

- vivid,
- flexible.

But the terms he lists for *monotone* include:
- drones and chants,
- lacks animation,
- sing-song,
- dull to listen to,
- bored,
- no enthusiasm.

These terms make it clear that you want to avoid using a monotone. When you use varied inflections, you can convey your enthusiasm for your job, your belief in your product/service, your interest in the prospect/customer.

If you have a tendency to speak in something of a monotone, you can listen to other TSRs to develop an awareness of how inflections can add color and life to a voice. Although largely an automatic response, inflections are something that can be practiced with effectiveness. Taping your side of conversations and listening to them will help you monitor your progress.

Sample Script

This script is a model for charitable organizations. It is aimed at potential corporate contributors. It is usually said almost word for word, and you will notice that it has some interaction. The reasons are the quantity of calls that are made and that it is a once-a-year contact. Also, many times volunteers do this kind of calling and they need a short, well-structured script to be able to stay on track and feel confident.

Hello, (prospect/customer's name). *This is* (your name), *a volunteer with* (organization). *I'm calling about the letter that we sent you last week. Do you have a couple of minutes?*

Thank you, (name).

As I mentioned, I'm calling about the letter we sent describing what (organization) does.

Many of our contributors have told us that they feel good about helping (organization), because 95 cents of every dollar they give stays in our community, helping our friends, neighbors and families. We know that each is managed responsibly and that our funds go for services that are not specified in the material we sent.

(Organization)'s goal for 19__ is $_____. We're giving high priority to safety education, home nursing care, and day care.

May I ask you a couple of quick questions?

Thank you. How many people do you have working for you? Fine. Is your company still located at (address)?

Many local firms have contributed to our organization's campaign. Would there be a possibility that your firm could donate $_____ per employee, or would a $_____ range per employee be closer to what you prefer.

Vocabulary

Inflection
Downward Inflection
Upward Inflection

Discussion Questions

1. When people speak on the telephone, they must use their voices for emphasis, because they do not have other options that people use in other settings—in face-to-face conversations or in writing. What are the techniques of emphasis that the voice is replacing?

2. What are the main ways of placing emphasis on the spoken word?

3. What are some benefits of using pauses in your telephone conversations?

4. What is a *creative* pause? When is it used? What does it accomplish?

5. Why do people "hem and haw" when they speak? What can this tell you about making your speech more effective?

6. What is a monotone? What does it say about the speaker?

7. Define inflection and cite the two basic kinds of inflection.

8. Describe the effects of ending phrases or sentences with each basic type of inflection. How are the two types like two different punctuation marks? How do they relate to telemarketing?

9. How do mixed inflections affect speech?

Activities

In all the activities listed here, you will be listening to tape recordings of yourself. However, the activities will be even more helpful if you and your classmates listen to one another's tapes and share ideas on what might be improved.

A. Emphasizing Your Words

For this exercise, make a tape of yourself describing a product/service or reading a sample script. Use the script at the end of this chapter if you prefer. You will play the tape twice. Have handy a list of ways of adding emphasis to speech:

Pausing before or after a word
Speeding up or slowing down
Holding a word or phrase
Changing pitch (giving inflection)
Raising or lowering volume

As you listen, check each kind of emphasis each time you hear it, to determine what kinds of emphasis you use most. Do you tend to use one or two over and over? Do you avoid a particular kind? Play the tape again, stopping it from time to time if necessary as you write down the words or sounds you emphasized, along with the kind of emphasis.

Decide whether your emphases were effective. Might you have used a different kind in a particular spot? Why? Should you use some kinds of emphasis that you do not usually use? Might you emphasize different words, place pauses differently? For what effect?

B. Punctuating With Pauses

Make a tape of yourself describing an event or a product/service. Then play the tape back, stopping when necessary so that you can write down each word and each sound—each "er" or "um"—. Now make another tape, repeating your speech but replacing each "er" or "um" with a silent pause. Play this tape back. What do the silent pauses achieve?

For a day, pay attention to the "er" and "um" sounds that you hear as people speak to you. Try to repeat to yourself (out loud if possible) the sentences you heard with "er" or "um," then the same sentences with pauses. Do the pauses improve the sentences?

C. Varying Inflection

Again, play a tape of yourself reading a prepared script or describing a product/service. Stop the tape when you need to write down what you hear. Note whether each sentence ends with an upward inflection ↗ or a downward inflection ↘ (use arrows). Also indicate words that have mixed inflections (a *W* is a good symbol to use).

Now listen to the tape again and evaluate your inflections. Are you ending some sentences with a question mark—an upward inflection—even though they are supposed to be statements, not questions? Say those sentences out loud, with downward inflections. Are there few words marked with the *W* symbol? Try saying some words over, varying your inflections.

You can also join your classmates for this. Have each person write out two or three sentences, neutral or positive in nature (such as, "This program starts next week" or "The price is lower now than it was last month") and mark each sentence with an upward or a downward arrow, indicating that it should be spoken with an upward or a downward inflection at the end.

Fold up the papers and pass them around the class so that nobody has the paper he or she wrote. Then take turns reading the sentences aloud, with the indicated inflections, and discuss what happens. Can a person who is actually a bit shy about reading aloud to the class sound confident reading a statement that ends with a downward inflection? What effects do upward inflections have on positive or neutral statements?

What Is Listening?

Better Listening, Better Results

Internal Obstacles to Listening

External Obstacles to Listening

Helping Your Ears

Vocabulary

Discussion Questions

Activities

Chapter 12

Listening to Communicate

Upon completion of this chapter, you will be able to

- distinguish between *hearing* and *listening*,
- describe two ways listening improves communication,
- overcome internal obstacles to listening,
- overcome external obstacles to listening,
- use mind, body, hand, and mouth to improve listening.

You have learned many valuable concepts and techniques of telemarketing. You have learned, for instance, to prepare and use a telephone dialog prompter and a script, to choose words that fit a conversational, soft sell approach, and to use your voice effectively. While you keep all these important aspects of telemarketing in mind, you also want—always—to be tuned in to the person at the other end of the line. As Dean Rusk, a former secretary of state, once said:

- "One of the best ways to persuade others is with your ears—by listening to them."

To be a good listener you must tune in to the words, tones, feelings of your prospects/customers and respond appropriately. You want to assure them that you are paying attention and encourage them to talk, so that you can learn more about what they want, about what is likely to sell them on a product/service. And you need to remember what they say, so that you can act upon it. An important part of any communication is listening.

You will be a good listener—able to concentrate, assuring and encouraging to the other person, and able to remember what is said—when you give your ears some help. In this chapter you will learn what effective listening requires, what roadblocks to avoid and ways in which you can use other senses to help your ears listen.

What Is Listening?

Listening means interpreting and understanding the sounds that enter your ear. **Hearing** refers to the reception of those sounds, the physical act of hearing. According to Dr. Lyman K. Steil, developer of a listening program for the Sperry Corporation, listening is a four-part process. Its components are:

1. Sensing—Physically receiving the spoken message.

2. Interpretation—Asking what the speaker's words mean.

3. Evaluation or judgment—Weighing the information in the message and deciding how it will be used.

4. Response—Giving a verbal or visible reaction, to show whether the message has been understood.

Although the sense of *hearing* is something people are born with, *listening* is a learned communication skill. In this chapter you will learn techniques that will help you to be a good listener and to use your listening skills to be effective.

Listening to understand the meaning of what is being said is important to all aspects of life, and it is the life's blood of business. Only when people comprehend the messages sent by their bosses, co-workers, clients, and prospects/customers can business run smoothly and grow. Poor comprehension snags routine operations and decreases sales.

Listening to understand involves more than listening to the words. It involves interpreting all the aspects of voice and language that you have been studying. You must listen carefully to interpret the speaker's pitch, emphasis, tone, rate, volume, inflection, and choice of words. You learned how pauses put emphasis into your speech. You need to consider what pauses mean in the speech of your prospect/customer.

Pauses provide signals. A prospect/customer might pause to think about a particular feature of a product/service and envision how it could be of help. Such a pause is a buying signal. You want to pick up on it, and make a suggestion relevant to what the prospect/customer is thinking about, not distract the prospect/customer by moving briskly on to describe some other, unrelated feature of the product/service.

Just as your rate and volume convey messages, so do the rate and volume of the prospect/customer at the other end of the telephone line. Loud volume? Maybe the prospect/customer is irritated. Fast rate? Maybe the prospect/customer is feeling rushed. You need these messages so you can respond appropriately—and to get these messages, you listen.

In much the same way as you make up for the lack of body language when you speak over the phone, you also make up for its absence as you listen. You cannot see your prospects/customers shake their heads, frown or smile. Instead, you listen to their voices for clues to their positive or negative feelings.

Be sure you are not so busy tuning in to the words that people are using that you miss the sense of what they are saying.

Better Listening, Better Results

In any conversation between two people, both people need the opportunity to speak. Telemarketing, you have learned, includes both inbound and outbound calls, and although they are different in character, both require good listening skills.

In inbound calls, prospects/clients often do most of the talking as they get a point across or make their wishes known. Effective TSRs listen carefully to determine what point the prospect/customer is making, what information is requested, what service is needed.

In *outbound* calls, when a prepared dialog prompter is used rather than a script, the interaction between the TSR and the prospect/customer is almost even. The TSR does most of the talking in the opening step. In the fact-finding step, the prospect/customer talks more. The TSR again has the floor during the persuasion step. Then the prospect/customer leads as he or she voices an opinion or gives an objection. The TSR listens intently to determine which step of the sale the prospect/customer is in mentally.

> The talkative listen to no one, for they are ever talking. The first evil that attends those who know not how to be silent is that they hear nothing.
>
> Plutarch c. 50-c.120

Listening to Have a Conversational Approach

You have learned that a conversational approach to telemarketing is most effective. As part of that approach, you want your telemarketing calls to be like natural, friendly conversations, with each person doing some talking, some listening. You want conversations that go back and forth, that have give and take.

"Listen more; communicate better," is the advice of John Croxall of Mutual Fund Associates in San Francisco. "Too many sales people are poor listeners. They think they have to keep talking, both on the phone and in an interview. The salesperson who engages in active listening can draw the prospect out and find out how he likes to be treated as a person; he finds out what the prospect thinks, how he feels, and how he responds," Mr. Croxall says. An anonymous speaker put it this way:

- *The more we listen, the more we sell.*

Listening for Feedback

Listening is essential in telemarketing because it is the only way for you to obtain a vital ingredient—*feedback*. You need feedback from the other person so that you will know what to do next, what approach to take. Even if you have extensive knowledge of your product/service—and truly believe in your product/service—you cannot operate *only* on your own knowledge and belief.

You need to know what prospects/customers think and feel. You learn this from feedback—by giving them the opportunity to speak. You learn by listening.

> It is the province of knowledge to speak and it is the privilege of wisdom to listen.
>
> Oliver Wendell Holmes
> 1809-1894.

Getting feedback lets you confirm meanings, make sure a word or phrase is understood, reduce misunderstandings, answer questions of the prospect/customer, and pick up on a prospect/customer's interest.

Internal Obstacles to Listening

We think faster than we speak and that is the first internal obstacle to good listening. Because your mind is working faster than the other person is talking, it has time to wander. No matter how interested you are in your work, miscellaneous thoughts about unrelated subjects—both serious and trivial—can pop into your mind for this reason. Suddenly you will think of an ill friend, your weekend tennis game, an errand you must run, or the approaching deadline for the big project in your office.

You can, however, take steps to reduce disjointed, distracting thoughts and to increase your listening effectiveness. You will read later in this chapter how to use your imagination, body language, hands, and your mouth to help you concentrate on what is being said and avoid having your mind wander.

The Clutter Obstacle

Mind clutter—the swirling, distracting thoughts that are unrelated to the task at hand—will make listening harder. If you are not feeling well or maybe had a late night the night before, you may have to make a special effort to concentrate and prepare yourself well for each call you make. Recall the discussion in Chapter 5 on clutter. Physical clutter—unnecessary papers and objects in your work area—will also make it harder to concentrate on listening to your prospect/customer.

Anticipation

Anticipation—that is assuming you know what the person is going to say—is another major internal roadblock. Once you begin anticipating, you stop really listening because you *know* what the person is going to say. When, as often happens, the person says something that you did not expect, you do not hear it at all. *Anticipation* is something TSRs must constantly guard against. They know their topic and after many calls know, to a great extent, what people will say in certain situations, and, as a result, it is all too easy for them to anticipate. This challenge is particularly acute when learning a person's name. For example, many common names, such as Smith, can have various spellings and pronunciations. The TSR who anticipates might not hear the right spelling or pronunciation.

External Obstacles to Listening

Concentration, patience, and interest are all abilities that you can develop along with the techniques described later to overcome internal roadblocks to listening. There will be times, however, when external conditions beyond your control create a situation where you simply cannot listen well. Examples of these conditions include the following:

- A poor connection. You might hear a buzzing, echo, another conversation, or the other person's voice may simply not be coming through loud enough even though he or she is speaking in a normal voice.

- A speaker phone, a portable or cellular phone such as in a car, sometimes does not transmit very clearly.

- Office background noise. There might be noise from an office machine such as a copier or hole punch or from construction work. TSRs working in offices in congested urban areas might even be disturbed by street noise, such as fire sirens or construction.

Although you may not have direct control over these external obstacles, you can still overcome them. If you have a poor connection you are better off acknowledging it right away rather than struggling through an entire call. It could become annoying to the prospect/customer if you have to keep asking them to repeat. Instead simply say:

- *Excuse me, (name), we seem to have a poor connection. Would you please hang up, and I will call you right back.*

Sometimes the connection is poor only for one of the two parties. If you sense that the person you are talking with is straining to hear you, you might ask:

- *(Name), is my voice coming through clearly? If not, perhaps we have a bad connection. Why don't you hang up and I will call you right back.*

> An old comic routine tersely sums up the need to be a good listener as well as a good talker to have successful communications. When two friends met on the street one day one of them had a noticeable black eye.
>
> First friend: Say, how did you get such a black eye?
>
> Second friend: I was *talking* when I should have been *listening*.
>
> You are in no danger of ever getting a black eye while talking on the telephone; but if you do all the talking and don't know when or how to listen, you will

Obviously you want to avoid suggesting that the person has a hearing problem.

Any office that is serious about its telemarketing program will put its TSRs in as quiet a location as possible and give them headsets to block out background noise and improve listening. You might even be assigned a soundproof work station. However, if there should be distracting background noise, it could affect your work. In such a case, speak to your manager.

Helping Your Ears

You can help your ears to hear and improve your listening ability by using your mind's eye, body language, your hands, and even your mouth.

Your Mind's Eye

Using your mind's eye is one way to improve your concentration. Although you cannot actually see the person at the other end of the telephone line, you can use your mind's eye to create clear mental images of the conversation. You can visualize what is being said—for instance, you can visualize the product/service in use—and you can imagine that you are seated with the person on the other end of the wire. Creating such images will help keep your mind off distracting thoughts and focused on the conversation.

Body Language

You can also use your body language to help you pay attention and respond to the person on the other end telephone line. Of course your listener cannot see your body language, however, as you learned, body language can affect the way you speak. It can also affect the way you listen. You want to feel comfortable when you listen, and using your natural body language helps you. You may smile as you share an idea, shake your head in concern when a prospect/customer describes a problem. Such movements help you to be at ease and to tune in to what is being said.

Your Hands

Can your hands help you to listen? Yes, when you use them to take notes. Clear, readable notes are essential to many professionals, including telemarketers. They provide you with a way to remember what was said and other benefits as well. Taking notes is in addition to keeping your regular records, which you must do as a matter of routine. Often, you hear information that is not part of the regular records, yet you nevertheless want to remember it. You cannot remember all that your prospects/customers tell you. Only by taking neat, accurate notes can you recall what you need. When you have the information at your fingertips, you will be efficient and professional in telemarketing.

Reasons to Take Notes

Taking notes can assist you in other ways as well. The following sections describe ways in which taking notes helps you be a more effective listener.

Helps Maintain Your Attention

When you take notes, your mind is less likely to wander and more likely to retain information. Without notes to refer to, you may be faced with asking prospects/customers to repeat something. When you do that, the prospects/customers are all too likely to think that:

- You were not listening.
- You were not interested in what they said.
- You do not care about them.
- You are bored with your job.
- You are not well informed about your product/service.

Frees Your Mind

By taking notes, you are better able to tune in to your prospects/customers' tones, hear their emphases, figure out what they are thinking. When you need to respond with a lower volume, to calm an irritated prospect/customer, you can concentrate better on doing that.

Helps With Inquiries or Complaints

When you take notes as prospects/customers ask questions or register complaints, you will find it easier to determine what they need to know or what must be corrected. Often your notes are what keep you from losing a prospect/customer.

Increases Sales

Taking notes helps you concentrate on the prospect/customer's signals, analyze needs, recognize hidden objections, and close sales. It helps you to be informed, relaxed and productive.

Your Mouth

Some of your talking will assist you in listening, for it will keep the prospects/customers talking, and thus give you more opportunity to learn by listening. You want your prospects/customers to let you know what they want, why they might consider your product/service, when they are ready to buy.

You can encourage your prospects/customers to keep talking by showing your interest in what they have to say. You can do that by making brief comments that indicate that you are listening and that you are interested. You can also encourage your prospects/customers to talk by asking them questions.

When you take these steps, you are being a good listener. And, by making your questions low-key and courteous, you will be taking a soft sell rather than a hard-sell approach. Your sales conversations will resemble easy conversations between friends, rather than high-pressure sales pitches.

Show Interest

You know what it is like to call a friend, relate your news, and then realize that you have not heard a sound from the other end of the line for some time. You stop and ask, "Joe, are you still there?" Joe, it turns out, *is* there. As you spoke, he was listening, nodding his head in agreement, smiling at your comments. Had you been face-to-face, you would have known that he was listening.

Over the phone, however, a speaker does not know that the listener is still there—and interested—unless the speaker makes audible responses. As a TSR, you need to make such responses when listening to your prospects/customers.

You want your responses to encourage, not distract, your prospect/customer. You need only to use short words and phrases. You do, however, want to be careful not to use the same one or two phrases over and over, for that is noticeable and distracting. Everyone knows somebody who cannot carry on a conversation without saying something like "Ya know?" several times.

Using a variety of short, audible responses helps you to sound like a professional with a good vocabulary and like a person who is interested. Most short, audible responses (Such as, "Oh, I see...") can be used in many different situations. Each such response triggers different inflections, and the variety, both of words (even all-purpose words like "right" or "really") and of inflections, makes your comments sound genuine and tailor-made to the listener.

Ask Questions

Knowing when to ask questions, knowing what kind to ask, and picking up on responses to the questions all require careful listening. And, in turn, asking the questions actually helps you to listen—to focus, to tune in.

Ask polite, low-key questions to find out what your prospects/customers are thinking and whether what you have said is clear to them. Asking questions shows that you are listening and helps them listen as well. Both your listening and the prospect's listening is necessary. When asking questions, however, avoid making it sound as if you are interrogating the prospect or pushing ("Why don't you want to sign up?"). However, do not miss opportunities, allow misunderstandings to stand, or leave doubts in the prospect's mind. (See the box on page 212 for a list of possible general questions.)

When you ask questions and listen to the answers carefully, you:

- show your interest in the person speaking,
- get to know your prospects/customers,
- maintain the prospect/customer's attention by giving them an opportunity to talk, (when a person is involved, he or she is usually more interested),
- stimulate the other person's thinking,
- make the other person more willing to listen to you,
- control the conversation.

Remember, as you learned in Chapter 2, there are three kinds of questions to ask during the fact-finding step of the sale, to help you learn the needs and wants of your prospects/customers:

- questions to learn about their background and situation,
- questions to learn what dissatisfactions, changes and challenges they face, and
- trial-closing questions to learn if you have an understanding of what your prospect/customer needs or wants.

From asking the first two kinds of questions, you *may* have an understanding of what your prospect needs or wants. This understanding will help you to decide exactly what features and benefits of your product/service you will describe as you move into the step to persuade your prospect to buy.

However, what you think the prospect wants or needs may not be correct. Even if you have been listening carefully, you may be thinking one thing while the prospect is thinking something else. You want to make sure that you are on the right track before you try to persuade prospects to buy something that they do not want or need. You need to determine their main interests—the features and benefits that they do want and need—first.

You do this by asking a trial-closing question. Only by checking and listening can you determine whether a prospect is ready to buy the features and benefits of a particular product/service or agree to arranging an appointment. If your prospect answers these questions in a positive way ("In my opinion, that is a really helpful feature") or chooses one of the choices you present ("Probably the larger model would be more useful"), then you can be certain you have correctly determined his or her main interest in the product/service. You can then move into the step to persuade.

However, if your prospects give negative answers ("In my opinion that is unnecessary") or reject the choices that you present ("Vinyl coated? Aluminum coated? No, I really don't like either"), they show their lack of interest. You need to ask more questions to find out what their interest is.

In all of this your ability to listen to the answers to your questions will help you keep on top of the conversation, evaluate the situation and make the right decisions as to which step of the sale to move into next.

Handle Objections

Part of the process of listening in telemarketing—in fact, in any sales conversation—involves hearing the prospects/customers' objections, determining what they mean, and responding appropriately to them. You will hear both general objections and specific objections. Listen carefully to be sure you know what kind of objection you have heard, because the kind of objection will determine your response.

For example, if general objections are raised, it may indicate a need to find out more about the prospect/customer's wants and needs, in which case you would courteously return the conversation to the fact-finding step. Specific objections, on the other hand, can be a strong buying signal, and could be a signal to begin moving to the closing, first by answering the objections.

GENERAL OBJECTIONS	SPECIFIC OBJECTIONS
I'm not interested	*I don't know if front-wheel drive*
No money	*is really what I need for my type*
The price is too high	*of driving.*
I'm too busy	*I don't think I need that much*
No time	*coverage. I already have*
	$100,000.

Listen for Clues

If you receive a general objection during any step of a sale, you know that the prospect/customer has not become interested by your initial benefit statement of the features and benefits of your product/service. In this case, there are steps you can take.

- You can try to find out just what would interest your prospect/customer. After your prospect/customer registers the objection, you can use a cushioning phrase (such as, "I understand"), answer the objection, and then ask more fact-finding questions. Then you will know better what features and benefits to focus on.

- You may decide simply to stimulate the prospect/customer's interest in the product/service by briefly describing more features and benefits. Before you do this, however, be sure to use a cushioning phrase and answer the objection.

- If you hear a general objection to a closing question, you may need to end the conversation—for now. After you have customized and answered their objection, be sure to leave the door open for another call. Do not try to apply pressure, for then the door might never be open to you again. A non-pressure closing that leaves the door open would be something like this: "Yes, timing isn't always right. However, since things have a way of changing, may I call back in..., just to touch base?" (Usually in three months.)

- A specific objection given during the first step of a sale—the opening—can be considered a buying signal. Such an objection indicates that the prospect/customer has heard what you are offering; otherwise, he or she could not raise a specific objection. However, prospects/customers may have received misinformation. You will have to clear that up by using a cushioning phrase and answering the objection. Always get prospects/customers' permission to ask questions; find out what they think they know about your product/service. Sometimes misinformation is the only thing that makes them hesitate to buy.

- A specific objection during the second step of the sale—during the fact-finding step—can also be considered a buying signal. People are not likely to waste their time raising specific objections unless they have some interest in what is being offered. A prospect/customer who raises a specific objection during your fact-finding may be trying to say, "Hey, this is a product/service I might like to buy. Please quit asking questions and tell me more about it."

And you will want to do just that after you have used a cushioning phrase and answered the objection.

- Finally, a specific objection given during the third or fourth step of a sale—persuasion and closing—when you are describing features and benefits or asking trial-closing questions—is not only a buying signal, but a hot buying signal. People are protective of their time, and those who are still listening and responding during the third or fourth step are definitely interested even if it is not for right now. You would, in the third and fourth step, use a cushioning phrase, answer the objection, and then move on to the trial closing or closing statement. In the fourth step, you might need only to use a cushioning phrase, answer the objective, and prepare to close.

Asking questions is part of listening. Both questions that can be answered with "yes" or "no" ("Do you need more information on that?") and "open-ended" questions that invite longer responses (Such as, "What do you think about this plan?") are useful. Asking questions like the ones listed here will help you in listening to your prospects/customers.

1. *Are you comfortable with that, or would you like me to go into more detail?*
2. *Do you see what a difference that would make?*
3. *How do you think that would work for you?*
4. *Can I add something to clarify that?*
5. *Please tell me how your present _____ works.*
6. *Do you have any questions?*
7. *Do you follow what I'm saying so far?*
8. *How does this sound to you?*
9. *How do you feel about that?*
10. *Is there anything else you'd like me to go over?*
11. *What do you think about that?*

Listen for Types

Different personality types have been identified, and listening carefully will help you to recognize the types and help you decide how to meet the specific objections of each prospect/customer.

Some people might be called "dominant," and dominant people usually make decisions quickly and stick with them. Others might be called "susceptible." They too make quick decisions. But they may regret their decision and return the product later. (It often helps to call such people after the sale to assure them that they have made the right decision. You might, for instance, call to point out extra features that they might not have noticed or simply to see how they like it or how it works for them.)

Others are "careful." They are careful decision-makers; they need time to think things over and may need to be contacted several times before they decide to buy something. Still others are "conservative." They are even more careful decision-makerdecision-makers and require a number of contacts.

A buying decision is different for each kind of decision-maker. It is a quick, definite "yes" for a dominant person, a "yes, but" to one who is susceptible. These two use the sentence "I have to think it over" mostly as a put-off. However, with careful or conservative people, the sentence "I have to think it over" may represent a buying decision. It is not a put-off, not an objection. They *have* to think it over to buy anything.

During a telesales conversation, dominant and susceptible people usually seem decisive and ask few questions. Careful and conservative people require many contacts; however, once they become customers, they will probably be loyal, and remain your customers as long as they are satisfied with your product/service.

It takes careful listening to decipher objections, to recognize what they mean, and what the prospect/customer is actually thinking.

Vocabulary

Anticipation
Hearing
Listening

Discussion Questions

1. Describe the difference between hearing and listening.

2. List and describe four components of listening.

3. Why is listening so important to telemarketing?

4. Listening to understand involves more than listening to the words a person uses. Explain.

5. What vital ingredient to telesales can a TSR obtain only by listening?

6. What internal obstacles can prevent good listening?

7. Describe three external obstacles to listening. What are some things you can do to overcome them?

8. How does your mind's eye help you to listen?

9. How can your body language help you to listen?

10. Name several benefits that taking notes provides.

11. Can some objections actually be buying signals? Explain.

Activities

These activities are designed to help you increase your listening effectiveness by using the techniques described in the text.

A. Using Your Mind's Eye

Call a friend and ask that friend to describe a recent experience—a trip to the supermarket or dentist, a project at work, a tennis game. Have ready a card with tone, volume, rate, and emphasis written on it.

As your friend speaks, jot down brief descriptions, such as "fast" for rate, "excited" for tone. After the call, think about it, study the card, and write down what you learned—including what your friend did not actually tell you, in words. Was the experience stressful or pleasant for your friend? Was your friend smiling or frowning while talking? How could you tell?

As your friend speaks, picture the events to yourself. You might want to jot down a few key words or phrases, or even draw a sketch of some important aspect of the story. When your friend has finished, repeat the description in your own words, but add the information you derived from nonverbal factors such as pitch, rate, and tone. Ask your friend to check the accuracy.

B. Listening for Buying Signals

Make a list of about five statements that you would use to describe the features and benefits of your product/service. Now pair up with a partner. Read the first statement on the list, then let your partner respond. If you say, "This service is available weekly," perhaps your partner will say, "I don't need it every week." Decide what to say to your partner's particular response. Perhaps you would use a trial-closing statement and say, "Monthly service could also be arranged if you prefer that."

Now, read the same statement again, and ask your partner to make a different response—maybe, "I don't think I can afford that"—or the same response but in an entirely different tone—hesitant, perhaps, or annoyed. What will you say this time? Take turns reading statements and giving different—or different-sounding—responses, to learn how important it is to listen to feedback.

As you read in the text, specific objections are often buying signals. Make a list of a half dozen questions related to the product/service you have been describing. Include both questions that verify that the prospect/customer understands you ("Do you see how these can be arranged?") and questions that help you to know what the prospect/customer is thinking ("What days are best for your office?"). When your partner gives a specific objection that you think is a buying signal, use one of these trial-closing questions. The more you get used to asking trial-closing questions, the easier closings will become.

Glossary

Add-on Suggestion (CP): *Suggestion selling* option used to increase sales dollar volume by suggesting an accessory that is not necessarily related to the initial purchase. See *tie-in suggestion*. (3)

Affirmation: The act of suggesting something definite and specific to yourself in a regular, systematic, and positive way so as to program your subconscious mind to create a positive attitude. Also known as *autosuggestion*. (6)

    Activity Affirmations: Affirmations you have recorded to listen to. These can be self-made affirmations or borrowed affirmations.

    Borrowed Affirmations: Affirmations based on material discovered in other sources.

    Self-made Affirmations: Positive statements you think up for yourself.

    Verbal Affirmations: Spoken or thought expressions of positive encouragement—affirmations in words.

    Visual Affirmations: Visual aids to help program your mind—positive, motivational pictures, clippings, drawings, or awards and ribbons, such as special people you admire or places you have been or would like to go. (6)

Anticipation: Assuming you know what the person is going to say. (12)

Appointment Call (CP): Call made to secure appointment to meet with the prospect/customer by phone or in person. One of the five basic types of telemarketing call. There are two types of appointment securing call: *with qualification* and *without qualification*. (2)

    Appointment securing with qualification: TSRs

ask questions about personal possessions, finances, and so on to determine whether to seek an appointment for the face-to-face salesperson. (3)

Appointment securing without qualification: TSRs simply secure an appointment without asking any qualifying questions. (3)

Articulation: As used in this text, the act of producing sounds clearly, distinctly and smoothly. Also known as *enunciation*. Compare *pronunciation*. (8)

Attention Span: The length of time a person can concentrate on what is being said. (4)

Autosuggestion: See *affirmation*. (6)

Benefit: What a particular *feature* gives the prospect/customer: savings in time or money, convenience or ease of use, efficiency, increased capacity for work, and so on. (2)

Bonus: Extra payment for reaching a certain goal. TSRs often receive bonuses and *commissions*, in addition to their regular salary or wage, to motivate performance. (2)

Call Activity: Specific content of each individual call—purposes and results—as opposed to general information. Compare *call information*. (7)

Call History Sheet: Index cards or sheets of paper on which are recorded the *call history* for each account. (7)

Call History: Record of all the *call information* and *call activity* for each account, from the time of the first call. (7)

Call Information: General information about a call—time, length of call, name of person called—as opposed to specific content. Compare *call activity*. (7)

Call Purpose: The identified reason for making a call; the goal or objective to be accomplished by a call. Also known as a *telemarketing application*. Note: call purposes defined in this glossary are all marked *CP*. (2)

Primary Purpose: The reason for a call. Can be any one of the many telemarketing applications. (3)

Secondary Purpose: Another topic to discuss—a related product, a higher grade product, an upgrade or sale—once the primary purpose has been covered. Used to increase the marketing potential of the call. (3)

Call Tracking Form: Form used to record the number of calls made in a day, how many contacts were made, what products or services were sold, what appointments were made, and any other information needed for the particular telemarketing application. (7)

Call-in Inquiry: Call for information, literature, or to place an order. (1)

Catalog Sales Call (CP): *Outbound call* to obtain permission to send a catalog and, subsequently, permission to call the prospect/customer on a regular basis; or *inbound call* responding to the catalog. (3)

Closing Question: Question which definitively asks the prospect for a commitment to buy or lease the product/service, to arrange an appointment, or to buy into an idea. See *trial-closing question*. (2)

Closing: Usually refers to making the sale: *closing* the deal. However, even asking permission to call the prospect back is a kind of selling—selling the idea of talking again. In this sense, every telemarketing call ends with a closing of some kind. Step IV of the sale. See *ending, Fact Finding, Opening, Persuading*. (2)

Cold Call: A call made without a prior appointment. (2)

Commission: Percentage of the total amount of the sale. TSRs often receive commissions and *bonuses*, in addition to their regular salary or wage, to motivate performance. (2)

Connotation: Subtle differences among the meanings of various words that can significantly alter the effect of your message. (8)

Consumer Response Call (CP): See *direct response call*. (3)

Context: Generally, the setting of a word, statement, idea, practice, etc. In this text, context refers to how and when a word is used in a given situation. (8)

Contraction: Two words combined into one: Will not = won't, Did not = didn't, You are = you're. (9)

Credit Application Solicitation Call (CP): Call made to encourage prospects/customers to apply for credit or charge cards. (3)

Cross-sell Suggestion (CP): *Suggestion selling* option used when a prospect/customer initiates a call but does not purchase the call-in interest item. The TSR suggests an alternate item that is unrelated to the original item. See *add-on suggestion*. (3)

Cushioning Technique: Positive response to complaints that projects a helpful, positive reaction. (6)

Customer Account Management: The process of servicing and keeping a large, strong *customer base*. There are three types of customer account management: complete account management, major/marginal account management, and credit account management. (2)

Customer Base: All the current customers a company has. (2)

Direct Mail: Brochures, letters or other material mailed directly from the company to the prospect/customer. (1)

Direct Method: Use of marketing tools and techniques to generate leads, to heighten the prospect/customer's acceptance level for outbound calls, and to encourage prospects/customers to make inbound calls. See *indirect method*. There are two uses of the direct method: *outbound* and *inbound*.

The **outbound direct method** employs a traditional marketing tool, such as a note of introduction in a letter or flyer, to inform the prospect/customer of a proposed call and its primary purpose.

The **inbound direct method** uses a traditional marketing tool, such as *direct mail* or *media advertising*, to encourage prospects/customers to make a call to place an order for a product/service or to seek information. (3)

Direct Response Call (CP): *Inbound call* made by a prospect who has been interested by a direct marketing method. After the initial purpose has been completed, *suggestion selling* is used to increase the volume of the sale. Also known as a *consumer response call*. (3)

800 Number: Toll free number used often for inbound telemarketing calls). (1)

80/20 Rule: Rule formulated by Vilfredo Pareto, a 19th century Italian economist, according to which the significant elements in any grouping make up only 20 percent of the total. Thus, 20 percent of your effort will bring in 80 percent of your results. (2)

Ending: The actual completion of the call—saying "Good-bye" and hanging up the phone—as opposed to the *closing*. (2)

Enunciation: See *articulation*. (8)

Esophagus: Food pipe leading to the stomach. (8)

Evocative: Evoking, or drawing out in the listener's imagination, the appealing qualities of an object. (8)

Fact Finding: The process of determining the prospect/customer's needs, wishes, history, and current situation, in order to know which product/service is appropriate and how it can best be presented. Step II of the sale. See *Closing, Opening, Persuading.* (2)

Feature: Something the product/service is, has, does, provides or uses that makes it special and valuable. See *benefit*. (2)

Feeling Question: Question designed to find out how the prospect/customer is feeling about the product/service. A form of *trial-closing question*. (2)

Follow-up: Making subsequent calls, with the prospect's permission, to keep in touch with the prospect/customer, and to address specific needs he or she may have. (2)

Free Gift Offer (CP): Offers a prospect a free gift for using a product or service, or for agreeing to an appointment for a demonstration or presentation. (3)

Free Trial Offer (CP): An offer to try out a product and to think it over. (3)

Fund Raising (CP): Outbound call in which TSRs or volunteers make calls to selected prospects and sell them on the idea of giving a donation. Can also be inbound call encouraged by radio or television pleas. (3)

Hearing: The physical act of hearing, the reception of sounds. See *listening*. (12)

Human Resources Configuration: The way in which a company organizes its TSRs' activities, such as *inside only, one person; telemate system*, etc. (3)

Human Resource Management: Selecting the appropriate *human resources configuration* for the telemarketing strategy being used. (3)

Idea Call: A call made to convince prospects to try something. One of the five basic types of telemarketing call. (2)

In-house Telemarketing: Telemarketing done by a company itself, rather than by another company hired for that purpose (see *Telemarketing Service Bureau*). (1)

Inbound Call: Call made by the prospect/customer to place an order, seek information, register a complaint, or conduct some other business. Also known as a *reactive call* because the company representative receiving the call reacts to the caller by taking appropriate action. (1)

Indirect Method: Suggestion of another product or service in addition to the specific one that was the reason for the call. Used as a *secondary purpose* to increase sales dollar volume and to stimulate interest in a product/service so as to develop the purpose for the next call. Also known as *suggestion selling*. (3)

Inflection: The raising or lowering of the *pitch*.
  Downward Inflection: Ending the word on a lower note.
  Upward Inflection: Ending the word on a higher note, so as to punctuate a sentence with a spoken "question mark." (11)

Initial Benefit Statement: Brief description of the product/service and one of its most important characteristics. Usually one sentence with enough information to interest the prospect. See *benefit*. (2)

Inside Sales: Sales done in the company, including both in-house telemarketing and other types of sales, such as that done by clerks in *retail* stores (see *outside sales*). (1)

Job Description: Summary of functions, tasks, and skills required in a job. (2)

Larynx: The human voice box at the top of the *trachea*. (8)

Lead Generation Project: Project designed to develop a list of prospective customers that can be called on later. (1)

Lead Qualification Call (CP): Call to prospects that have been identified through traditional marketing methods. The call is used to ascertain interest level of the person responding to the direct marketing method. (3)

Lead-in: A transitional question or comment to help the conversation flow smoothly through its various phases. (2)

Listening: Interpreting and understanding the sounds that enter your ear. Compare *hearing*. (12)

Loss Leader: A product that is being sold at a low price, probably no more than cost, on which the store does not make money. Used to lure customers into making further purchases. (3)

Maintenance Goals: Those activities that a group must carry out to exist—to maintain itself. (2)

Market Research: Making calls for information, rather than providing a service or making sales. (1)

Market Research Call: Call made to determine the marketing possibilities of a product or service. One of the five basic types of telemarketing call. (2)

Market Survey: Project in which many people are called and asked their opinion on a particular product or service to determine a potential market. (1)

Marketing: The effort to create a favorable atmosphere for the sale of a product or service. Compare *selling*. (1)

Media Advertising: Advertising in radio, television, newspapers, etc. (3)

Mind Clutter: Distracting material clouding the mind that is irrelevant to the calls you are making. (5)

New Product/Service Introduction Calls (CP): Calls to inform prospects/customers in a targeted area about a new product or service. (3)

Note of Introduction: Note or letter to prospects/customers informing them that they will shortly be receiving a call or visit. Notes of introduction include an 800 number to call for those who do not want to receive the call. (3)

Opening: The first few sentences at the beginning of a call, whether inbound or outbound. Highly variable, depending on the type of call being made or received. Step I of the sale. See *Closing, Fact Finding, Persuading*. (2)

Order Entry: Inbound call made by a customer to place an order for a product or service. (3)

Outbound Call: Call made by a TSR to a prospect or customer, to offer a product or service for sale, to arrange an appointment, to sell an idea, or to perform a business service. Also known as a *proactive call* because the company's representative takes the initiative to make the call. (1)

Outside Sales: Sales in which people make sales and service calls on the outside. See *inside sales*. (1)

Peripheral vision: Eyes' ability to perceive images not only in front but also from both sides. (5)

Persuading: The step of the sale during which the *features* and *benefits* of the product/service are described. Step III of the sale. See *Closing, Fact Finding, Opening*. (2)

Pharynx: Passageway used for both breathing and eating, through which food and air pass on their way to the stomach and lungs. (8)

Pitch: The lowness or highness of the voice in a musical sense: children's voices generally have a higher *pitch* than adults'. Compare *volume*. (10)

Presentation: The overall plan for carrying out a call. Standard sales presentations for telemarketing operations can be divided into seven parts—four steps of the sale (*Opening*, *Fact Finding*, *Persuading*, and *Closing*) and three related tasks (call preparation, *ending*, and record management). (2)

Proactive Call: See *outbound call*. (1)

Procedure: A set sequence of steps to follow. (5)

Products: Goods that belong to the customer once they have been sold. Products can be tangible, like furniture, appliances, or automobiles; or intangible, like insurance policies. Compare *service*. (2)

Product/Service Sales Call: Call to sell a *product* or a *service*. One of the five basic types of telemarketing call. (2)

Prompter: Outline of the prepared presentation. Gives key words and concepts to be conveyed, as opposed to exact wording. Compare *script*. (4)

Pronunciation: As used in this text, the standard, accepted sounds made in saying a given word. Compare *articulation*. (8)

Prospect Base: List of potential customers. (2)

Prospect Development: The process of building a large, strong *prospect base* and gradually converting prospects into customers by carrying out prospect *follow-up*. (2)

Pure Teleservice: See *Teleservice and Teleorder (no selling)*. (3)

Reactivating Old Accounts (CP): Call is to discover why the customer stopped doing business with the company, and, if possible, to renew the business relationship. (3)

Reactive Call: See *inbound call*. (1)

Record Management System: A computerized or manual way to compile a written record of all calls. (7)

Recruiting Call (CP): Application addressing a targeted market. People are asked to join an organization, such as the armed forces, a health club, a vacation club, to enroll in college, and so on. Recruiting calls can have either one of two primary purposes: to secure an *appointment* or to secure the commitment to join. (3)

Referral: Suggestion that the TSR call the person's friend, relative, or business associate about the product/service. (2)

Referral Follow-up Call (CP): Call using the name of a third party as a reference, like a referral in traditional sales. (3)

Reminder Calendar: A calendar in book form, with one day per page, on which you write, under the appropriate date, the names of prospects/customers you are to call. (7)

Retail: Stores that sell directly to consumers, as opposed to those that sell in bulk to other stores. (3)

Sales Call: Call made specifically to make a sale (as opposed to *service and order entry calls* and *market research calls*). Three of the five basic types of telemarketing call are sales calls: the *appointment call*, the *idea call*, and the *product/service sales call*. (2)

Sales: See *selling*.

Script: Written record of exactly what to say during a telemarketing call: questions to ask, suggestions to make. Compare *presentation* and *prompter*. (4)

Self-fulfilling Prophecy: An expectation that comes true because it is expected to come true. (6)

Selling: Direct efforts to sell a specific product or service to a specific prospect. Can include clerk in a store waiting on a customer, salesperson in a showroom, door-to-door or office-to-office salesperson, and telemarketing calls. Compare *marketing*. (1)

Service: Task performed by a company for a customer, either once or on a regular basis. Services are intangible but may involve the use of a *product*. (2)

Service and Order Entry Call: Any call a company makes or receives that helps a customer. Specifically, a call to help customers who have made a purchase or who want to make a purchase and have called to place an order, for information, or some other kind of help. Often a follow-up call to one a customer has made. One of the five basic types of telemarketing call. See also *Teleservice and Teleorder*. (2)

Service Contract: Contract under which the company agrees to maintain and repair the product for a specified amount of time. (3)

Softener: Phrase that ties each feature/benefit set together in a natural, casual, conversational way. (2)

Software: Computer programs. (7)

Strategy: Overall plan of action developed to accomplish clearly stated objectives. (3)

Subliminal: Unconscious; below the level of conscious perception. (8)

Suggestion Selling: See *indirect method*. (3)

Superlative: Word expressing the extreme degree of some condition. (8)

Survey Call (CP): Call to collect data on which to base marketing strategies or product/service offers. (3)

Tele-information Service (CP): A service that provides the customer with regular updates on new products or services, improvements, changes, sales, special opportunities, and so on. (3)

Teleaccount Executive: See *Teleaccount Representative*. (1)

Teleaccount Representative: A person who sells to and services a select group of customers. Also known as a *Teleaccount Executive*. (1)

Telecollection Call (CP): Planned reminder call made to keep accounts current. The purpose is to work out a payment arrangement. No selling is done on this call. (3)

Telecollector: A person who collects past due accounts by phone. (1)

Telemarketing Application: See *call purpose*. (3)

Telemarketing Service Bureau (TSB): A company created and organized to carry out telemarketing for others, which hires and trains workers to make and/or receive a wide variety of calls for different businesses. (1)

Telemate System: Use of two-person teams to generate and service accounts. (3)

Telemod: Sound-proof telemarketing stations used by some telemarketing operations. (1)

Telephone Sales Representative (TSR): A person who uses the phone to sell a product, service, or equipment. This includes people who make outbound calls, and people who receive inbound sales calls. (1)

Telephone Service Representative (TSR): A person who takes customer service and order entry calls or makes calls that are service-oriented. (1)

Telephone Sales/Service Representative (TSR): General title for anyone making or receiving sales or service calls. (1)

Telesales: Efforts to sell products and services, arrange appointments, and sell ideas. One of the four telemarketing career paths. (1)

Telesalesperson: A person who sells products/services by phone. (1)

Teleservice and Teleorder: Making or receiving *service and order entry* calls for customer service, such as taking orders, providing information, answering questions and giving assistance, handling complaints, and so on. This includes two of the four telemarketing career paths:
With no selling: Making or receiving *only* service calls. Also known as *pure teleservice* (3).
With selling: Service calls that can be expanded to include sales activity. (1)

Third Party Influence: An individual or group of people that has used and enjoyed the product/service. A way of presenting the *initial benefit statement* in a soft sell manner. (2)

Tie-in Suggestion (CP): *Suggestion selling* option used to increase sales dollar volume by suggesting an accessory that ties in with the initial purchase. See *add-on suggestion*. (3)

Tone: The emotional quality of a person's voice. Conveys feelings and attitudes; indicates whether the speaker is pleased or angered, enthusiastic or weary, friendly or hostile. (10)

Trachea: Air pipe leading to the lungs. (8)

Traffic Builder Call (CP): Call designed to increase the number of people who come to a place of business. Can be *outbound calls* made by the TSR, or *inbound calls* from the customer. (3)

Trial-Closing Question: Question in non-pressure, conversational language that allows the prospect/customer to express feelings on various options without making a commitment. Usually phrased in hypothetical terms to allow for flexibility. See *closing question*. (2)

TSR: Abbreviation that refers either to a *Telephone Sales Representative* or to a *Telephone Service Representative*. (1)

Up-sell Suggestion (CP): *Suggestion selling* option used to increase sales dollar volume by suggesting alternate choices of higher grades. See *tie-in* and *add-on suggestion*. (3)

Vocal Cords: The folds of tissue that close the *larynx*. When stretched tight, they vibrate, producing sound waves in the air coming from the lungs through the larynx, creating the sounds of the voice. (8)

Volume: Loudness or softness of the voice. Compare *pitch*. (10)

Index

Abbreviations, 125, 128 - 129, 141
Accountability, 39
Actors
    Memorizing scripts, 64
Add-on suggestion, 54
    Inbound call and, 31
Affirmations, 103 - 108, 113
    Activity, 106
    Borrowed, 105
    Defined, 103
    See also Positive attitude
    Self-made, 105
    Verbal, 105
    Visual, 106
"Ain't", 162
Amplification
    In telephones, 178
Annual Guide to Telemarketing, 44
Anticipation
    As listening obstacle, 204
Appointment call
    As outbound call, 9
    As sales call, 38
    Defined, 20
    With qualification, 53
    Without qualification, 52
Appointments, 16, 53, 58
    See also Appointment call
    arranging, 7, 160
    Record keeping for, 123
Articulation, 136, 146 - 149, 182
    See also Consonants
    Defined, 136
    See also Pronunciation
    See also Vowels
Attention span, 179
    Defined, 70
Attitude
    See Positive attitude

Autosuggestion
    See Affirmation
Backache, 177
Bell Systems, 3
Bell Telephone Alphabet, 83
Bell, Alexander Graham, 5, 11
Benefit
    Initial benefit statement, 28
Benefits, 32, 37, 55, 70, 107, 215
    Defined, 34
    See also Features
    Initial benefit statement, 27, 30
    Sample, 35
Body language, 169 - 170, 187, 206
Bonus
    See also Commission
    Defined, 18
    Telemate system and, 58 - 59
Breathing exercises, 180
Breathing system, 146
Buying signals, 107, 210 - 212
Call activity, 119 - 121, 126
    Defined, 118
Call history
    Defined, 120
Call history sheet, 119 - 123, 126
    Defined, 120
Call information, 120
    Defined, 118
Call preparation, 21, 131
Call purpose, 43, 48 - 55, 124
    Defined, 17
    Primary, 47, 55 - 56
    Secondary, 47 - 48, 55 - 56
    See also Telemarketing application
Call tracking form, 123 - 126
    Defined, 123
Call-in inquiry

Defined, 8
Career paths
    Call purposes and, 48 - 55
    Telemarketing call types and, 19
    Telesales, 7
    Teleservice and teleorder (no selling), 7
    Teleservice and teleorder (with selling), 7
Carnegie, Dale, 23
Catalog sales call, 52
Closing, 21, 35 - 36, 85
    Defined, 38
Closing questions, 34, 38, 107
    Defined, 36
    See also Trial-closing questions
Cold call
    Defined, 20
Commission
    See also Bonus
    Defined, 18
    In account management systems, 18
    In telemate system, 58
    Telemate system and, 59
Complaints, 49, 54, 108 - 112
    Fact finding and, 33
    Follow-up for, 108
    Preventing, 109, 111
    Procedure for, 88
    Rate of speech and, 179
    Record keeping for, 118, 129 - 130
    Steps for handling, 110
    Taking notes and, 207
    Volume and, 182
Computers
    For record keeping, 118
    Making calls, 5
    See also Software
    TSRs and, 119
Confidence, 18, 26, 172 - 173, 181, 191
    Affirmations for, 105, 107
    In closing, 36
    Working with secretary, 29
Connotation, 162
    Defined, 138
Conscious mind, 102, 104
    See also Subconscious mind
Consonants, 146 - 147, 149
    In abbreviations, 128

Consumer response call
    See Direct response call
Context
    Defined, 137
    Of words, 137 - 138
Contractions, 162
    Defined, 160
Conversational method, 70, 179, 199, 202
    See also Language, conversational
    See also Soft sell
Credibility
    Of company, 55
    Of descriptions, 137
    Of TSR, 108
Credit application solicitation call, 49
Cross-sell suggestion, 48, 55
Croxall, John, 202
Cushioning phrases
    See Cushioning technique
Cushioning technique, 108 - 110, 112, 211
    See also Transitional phrases
Customer account management, 17
    Complete, 17 - 18
    Credit, 17, 19
    Major/Marginal, 17 - 18
Customer base
    Defined, 17
Decision-maker, 22 - 25, 27 - 30, 37 - 38, 82, 84, 100 - 101, 123, 125, 213
Dictionary, 145
Direct mail, 38, 47, 56, 126
    Defined, 5
Direct method, 50, 56
    Defined, 55
    Inbound, 56, 125
    Outbound, 55
Direct response call, 52
Distractions, 78, 171 - 173, 178, 181, 205
    See also Listening, Obstacles
    Mispronunciations as, 145
    Reducing, 206
    Taking notes and, 207
800 numbers, 8, 31, 44, 88
80/20 rule, 18
Ending, 21, 85

Defined, 39
Enunciation
    See Articulation
Esophagus, 147
Extensions
    Procedure for, 87
Face-to-face communication, 82, 156, 171, 178
    Compared with telephone communication, 39
Face-to-face sales, 47, 57, 59, 98 - 99, 169, 172
    Cost of, 6
    In complete account management, 17
Fact finding, 21, 33 - 34
    Defined, 32
Fatigue, 177
    Mind clutter and, 80
Features, 32, 55, 68, 70, 188, 201
    See also Benefits
    Defined, 34
    Sample, 35
Feeling questions
    Defined, 35
    See also Trial-closing questions
Files
    See Record keeping
Fishman, Arnold L., 44
Follow-up, 17, 20, 50, 88, 122, 126, 130
    Complaints and, 108
    Defined, 16
Free gift offer, 51
Free trial offer, 51
Fund raising, 53
    As idea call, 20
    Sample script for, 193
Gestures
    See Body language
Grammar, 160, 162
Handicapped
    Job opportunities for, 6
Hard sell
    See Soft sell
Headsets, 78, 177
Hearing, 200
    See also Listening
Hold, 88
How to Put Yourself Across Over The Phone, 6
Human resource management, 58
Human resources configuration
    Defined, 57
    Inside only, 58
    Inside/Outside, 58
    See also Telemate system
Idea call
    As outbound call, 9
    Defined, 20
Inbound call, 9 - 11, 16, 23, 30, 48, 52 - 58, 124, 202
    Defined, 10
    In complete account management, 17
    Procedure for, 86 - 88
    Record keeping for, 118 - 119, 124 - 126
Indirect Method, 50
    Defined, 56
    See also Suggestion Selling
Individuality
    In language, 141
Inflection, 171, 188, 190 - 193, 208
    Customer's, 201
    Defined, 190
    Downward, 191
    See also Pitch
    Upward, 191
Informality
    See Conversational method
    See also Language, conversational
In-house telemarketing, 7 - 8, 58
    Cost of, 8
    Defined, 7
Initial benefit statement
    See Benefits
Inside sales
    Defined, 7
    See also In-house telemarketing
Inventory control, 125 - 126
Jargon, 141
Jaw movement, 182
Job description, 10
    Defined, 19
Kordahl, Eugene B., 4
Language, 135 - 144, 155
    See also Body language
    Comfortable, 161
    Context and, 136 - 138

Conversational, 23, 34, 71, 160 - 163
  Courteous, 142
  Customer's, 201
  Descriptive, 137 - 142
  Evocative, 141
  Formal, 160
  Negative, 143, 147
  Positive, 36, 143 - 144, 147
  See also Soft sell
  Specific, 137
  Technical, 141
Larynx, 147
Lead generation projects
  Defined, 8
Lead qualification call, 50
Lead-in, 31 - 32, 35
  Defined, 21
Leads, 52
Legislation
  To regulate telemarketing, 5
Ling, Mona, 6
Listening, 128 - 129, 170, 200 - 213
  Asking questions and, 33
  Complaints, 130
  Obstacles, 203 - 205
  Questions for, 212
Loss leader
  Defined, 51
Lungs, 147
Maintenance goals
  Defined, 16
  Of customer account management, 17
Maltz, Maxwell, 105
Management
  Overseeing telemarketing, 7
  Record keeping and, 117 - 118, 124
Market research
  As career path, 20
  Defined, 7
  Scripts in, 64
Market Research Call, 55
  Defined, 21
Market survey
  Defined, 8
  Sample script for, 71
Marketing, 21, 47, 50, 52, 55 - 56, 63, 126, 156
  As career path, 55
  Defined, 4

  See also Selling
  See also Suggestion Selling
Mayer, Lyle V., 192
Media advertising, 47, 56, 126
Mehrabian, Dr. Alfred, 169 - 170
Memory
  Steps to improve, 68
Mind clutter, 79 - 81, 203
Mind's eye, 172, 205
Minorities
  Job opportunities for, 6
Monotone, 190, 192
Mouthpiece, 78, 148, 178
Murray, Dr. Joseph, 105
Music, 174 - 175, 188 - 189
  See also Rhythm
Negative attitude, 98, 100 - 104, 108
  See also Positive attitude
New product/service introduction call, 50
Non-pressure language
  See Language, conversational
Note of introduction
  Defined, 47
  In reaching decision-maker, 29
Opening, 21 - 31, 106
  Customer's opening statement, 88
  Defined, 22
  Descriptive language in, 137 - 138
  Fake survey as, 55
  Of inbound call, 30
Order entry
  Defined, 54
  In telemarketing strategies, 45
  Record keeping for, 124
  With suggestion selling, 54
Outbound call, 9, 11, 16, 48 - 56, 58, 202
  Defined, 9
  Procedure for, 89 - 90, 92
  Record keeping for, 119 - 120, 122 - 124
Outside sales, 16, 58 - 59, 176
  Defined, 7
Pareto, Vilfredo, 18
Pauses, 188 - 190
  Before lead-ins, 145
  For emphasis, 171, 189
  For melodic rhythm, 171

Prospect/customer's, 201
   Verbalized, 190
Peripheral vision, 80
   Defined, 79
Personality types, 213
Persuading, 21, 34, 36
   Defined, 34
Pharynx, 146
Phonetic spelling
   See Spelling, phonetic
Pitch, 171, 175 - 178, 180 - 181, 188, 190
   Customer's, 201
   Defined, 174
   See also Inflection
Polite persistence, 17, 99, 131
Positive attitude, 97 - 108, 111 - 113, 143
   See also Affirmations
   Customer's, 109
   See also Language, positive
   See also Negative attitude
   Secretary's, 29
   Voice and, 172
   Working with secretary, 29
Power of the Subconscious Mind, The, 105
Presentation, 21, 65, 71, 91, 117, 126, 131
   See also Call preparation
   See also Closing
   Defined, 21
   See also Ending
   See also Fact finding
   Irritating words in, 162
   See also Opening
   See also Persuading
   Pronunciation in, 146
   See also Script
Proactive call
   Defined, 9
   See also Outbound call
Procedure, 66, 82 - 83, 85 - 92
   Defined, 81
   Inbound call, 86 - 89
   Outbound call, 89 - 91
Product
   Defined, 19
   Knowledge of, 63, 66, 68 - 69
   Record keeping and, 119
   Selecting, 32

   Service contract for, 49
   Used by customer, 33
   Word choice and, 136
Product/Service Sales Call
   Defined, 19
Prompter, 64 - 66
   Defined, 64
   In job description, 10
   Learning, 67
   Listening and, 202
   Preparing, 69
   Sample, 65
Pronunciation, 136, 145 - 146, 149
   See also Articulation
   Defined, 136
   Of names, 22 - 24, 83, 121, 126, 146
   Of words, 136, 145 - 146
Prospect base, 50
   Defined, 16
Prospect development
   Defined, 16
   In major/marginal account management, 18
Psychology, 16, 163
Punctuation, 188
   In speech, 189 - 190
Pure teleservice
   Defined, 54
Rate of speech, 178 - 181, 188
   Customer's, 201
Reactivating old accounts, 49
Reactive call
   Defined, 10
   See also Inbound call
Receiver, 78
Record keeping, 117 - 120, 122 - 126, 129 - 131
   Equipment, 119 - 125
   For complaints, 129 - 130
   For inbound call, 124 - 126
   For outbound call, 119 - 124
   Record management system, 118
Record management, 10, 21
Record management system
   See Record keeping
Recruiting call, 53
Referral follow-up call, 49
Referrals, 124
   Defined, 27
   See also Referral follow-up call

Reminder calendar, 121 - 122, 126, 130
   Defined, 120
Retail, 7, 51
Rhythm, 70
Sales
   See Selling
Sales call, 104
   As outbound call, 9
   Defined, 19
   Inbound, 11
   Product, 19
   Record keeping for, 124
   Service, 19
Sales conversation, 22
Schuller, Dr. Robert, 105
Screening calls, 88
Script, 66, 70 - 71, 81, 178, 199
   Defined, 64
   See also Presentation
   Sample, 71, 193
Self-fulfilling prophecy
   Defined, 102
Selling, 36, 48, 55, 156
   As primary purpose, 48
   Defined, 5
   Mail-order, 125
   See also Marketing
   See also Suggestion Selling
Service, 51
   Defined, 20
   Free introductory offer for, 50
Service and order entry call, 11
   As telemarketing, 57
   Career paths and, 20
   Defined, 20
Service contract, 49
Silence
   See Pauses
Slang, 162
Smoking, 78, 175 - 176
Soft sell, 26 - 29, 31, 36, 88, 107, 156 - 160, 170, 172, 191, 208, 211
Softener
   Defined, 35
Software, 118 - 119
Speech-producing system, 146
Spelling
   Name of caller, 86, 89
   Names, 23
   Phonetic, 83, 128

Steil, Dr. Lyman K., 200
Stone, W. Clement, 105
Strategy
   Development, 45
   Human resources configuration and, 58
   Implementation, 55
   In telemarketing, 44
Stress, 177, 180
   Preventing, 113
   Reducing, 130, 176 - 177
   See also Tension
Subconscious mind, 67, 101, 104 - 106, 108, 143
   See also Affirmations
   See also Conscious mind
   Peripheral vision and, 80
   Programming, 103
   Words and, 139
Subliminal efffects, 139
Suggestion selling, 48 - 51, 53 - 55
   Defined, 56
   See also Indirect method
Superlative, 188
   Defined, 140
Survey call, 55
Syllables
   Emphasis and, 187
   In abbreviations, 128
   Pitch and, 192
   Pronunciation and, 146
Synonyms, 138
Teleaccount Executive
   Defined, 11
Teleaccount representative
   Defined, 11
Telecollection call, 53
Telecollector
   Defined, 11
Telegraphic style, 127
Tele-information service, 50, 52
   Defined, 50
Telemarketer
   See TSR
Telemarketing application, 43, 48, 53, 57, 119, 123
   See also Call purpose
Telemarketing call
   Business-to-business, 16
   Business-to-consumer, 16
   See also Call preparation

See also Closing
See also Ending
See also Fact finding
Five basic types, 19
See also Opening
See also Persuading
Structure of, 21 - 39
Telemarketing service bureau, 8, 64
    Defined, 8
Telemate system, 58 - 59
Telemod
    Defined, 8
Telephone sales representative
    Defined, 11
Telephone service representative
    Defined, 11
Telesales, 45, 48, 135, 138
    Defined, 7
Telesalesperson
    Defined, 11
Teleservice and teleorder, 45, 48, 135
    No sales, 53
    With sales, 54
Tension, 67, 130, 175 - 176, 180
    Avoiding, 82
    Reducing, 176 - 177, 180
    See also Stress
Third party influence, 28, 30
    Defined, 27
Tie-in suggestion, 54
Time zones, 90
Titles
    In telemarketing, 11
Tone, 82, 86, 102, 141, 170 - 174
    Customer's, 108, 201, 207
    Defined, 172
    See also Inflection
    See also Pitch
Trachea, 147
Traffic builder call, 51
    Sample prompter for, 65
Transitional phrases, 21, 24, 31, 54, 56, 109, 145
    See also Cushioning technique
Trial-closing question, 34 - 38, 210, 212
Trial-closing questions
    See also Closing questions
    Defined, 34

See also Feeling questions
Trust, 18, 26, 33, 54, 100, 107, 190
TSR
    Abbreviations for, 125
    Advantages of, 172
    Articulation by, 146
    Body language and, 170
    Compared to actors, 66
    Complaints and, 130
    Defined, 11
    Giving speeches, 160
    Listening to, 193
    Memory of, 68
    Mispronunciation and, 145
    Record keeping by, 126
    Sample job description, 10
    Taking notes and, 206
    Tension and, 176
    Voice of, 171
TV telethons, 53
Unconscious mind
    See Subconscious mind
Up-sell suggestion, 54
Vocal cords, 147, 174 - 177, 189
Voice, 169 - 177, 180 - 182, 187 - 193
    As musical instrument, 175
    Caller's, 108
    Customer's, 201
    Distortions, 78
    Importance of, 174
    In handling complaints, 130
    Recognizing caller's, 85
    See also Tone
    When reading scripts, 68
Voice box
    See Larynx
Volume, 171, 174, 181 - 182, 188 - 189, 207
    Customer's, 201
    Defined, 180
Volunteers, 53
Vowels, 146 - 147
    In abbreviations, 128
Words
    See Articulation
    See Language
    See Pronunciation